When God Asks You...

How Will You Answer?

tom lemke

Grateful Ministry books may be ordered by contacting:

tom@gratefulministry.com

Bible Passages have been taken from the World English Bible (WEB) or King James Version (KJV) in the public domain.

Because of the dynamic nature of the Internet, any web addresses or links contained in this book may have changed since publication and may no longer be valid. The views expressed in this work are solely those of the author and do not necessarily reflect the views of the publisher, and the publisher hereby disclaims any responsibility for them. Any people depicted in stock imagery provided are models, and such images are used for illustrative purposes only.

ISBN: 979-8-9869259-0-5 (SC)

ISBN: 979-8-9869259-1-2 (e)
rev. date: 09/30/2022

Dedicated to the glory of God
and to my children, God's greatest gift to me.

Table of Contents

PART I

Do you open your eyes after a good sleep and think, "Wow, another day to live!"?

Do you ever take your first steps of the day and say, "I'm so grateful for a good back, strong legs, and the ability to walk without trouble today!"?

Do you fix your morning coffee or tea (or green smoothie) and greet the day with, "Can't wait to see what blessings God has for me this day!"

Neither did I, until that one day....

Chapter 1: Driving in a Fog

The morning fog obscured my view of the road ahead. I was confident in knowing where I was going, but I had slowed down. My Corvette, with headlights and fog lights on, moved steadily through the ground-level cloud toward my destination.

Driving to work, I went down the mental list of tasks for my day. I thought about my job had helped me to be right where I wanted to be-- moving ahead and developing new opportunities far beyond those in the Wisconsin town I'd grown up in. Now I was cruising through the big city streets in this beauty of a sportscar which proved to everyone how far I'd come in life.

I was brought back to the present by the blinking left-turn signal of a school bus headed my way on the two-lane highway we were traveling. The bus sat opposite me, awaiting an opportunity to turn safely across my lane.

I respected the bus driver's dilemma. After all, my father had owned a school bus business, and I had driven a school bus while in college. I thought about how glad I was that those days were behind me. No more trudging through dusty, pot-holed country roads in a massive bus, loaded with noisy kids. Now I could zip right through the streets in my two-passenger roadster. I could drive myself to where I wanted to be — in the middle of important transactions, shaking hands with big wigs, attending swanky parties. I wasn't a nameless chauffeur anymore. I had made a name for myself.

Still, I understood that busses were full of school children and therefore the driver must consider safety first. There is nothing more precious than a child's life.

My headlights shone through the fog to alert oncoming traffic that I was approaching. I trusted the bus was waiting on me to pass. Due to the fog, I had cut my speed from the usual 65 mph allowed on this road.

When I bought this car, the one thing that stuck in my mind was that it went from zero to sixty in just 8.4 seconds. It never crossed my mind to ask how fast it could stop.

I thought I was in control. But nothing could have prepared me for the impending obstruction ahead. Turning across my lane, the massive yellow school bus moved directly to where my car was careening at about 50 mph.

I jammed on the brakes, desperate to stop, NOW!

My car jerked to the right, sliding onto the shoulder, dipping into the roadside ditch, returning to the highway, and finally skidding toward the bus, broadside.

That's when time began to stretch, and everything started going in slow motion. The right side of the windshield crackled and sputtered, spidery-veined cracks and glinting shards spreading and popping toward me, reaching to grab hold of me. Every breaking chink sounded in my ears and in my mind, compounding my confusion. I seemed to be outside of myself, watching everything as if it were happening in a movie.

The next image I recall was the right rear corner bumper of the bus penetrating the windshield, smashing through the remaining thick glass meant to protect the driver—me. I saw the black bus bumper beneath the cautionary yellow metal thrusting itself further and further into my space, threatening to crush my skull.

Then, my memory went blank.

Everything was quiet. All was still. It was as if time had stopped.

Walking Away

I had no idea where I was. My hands were on the steering wheel, but I wasn't going anywhere. My body was in the car, but I was not sitting right. I was somewhat scrunched down in the driver's seat as if I had been trying to slide under that dashboard. It was as if I had been a child trying to squeeze myself into a special hiding spot during a game of hide-and-seek.

My adult frame measured 6 foot 3, and the Corvette driver's side didn't provide a great hideout.

My head hurt. Something warm and sticky was running down the side of my face.

I was confused. Something was speckling my head and shoulders. I noticed shiny blue specs the same color as my car all around me.

Gradually, I began to understand that I had been in a wreck.

The T-top roof panel from the roof's driver's side was resting on my head. The overhanging metal roof frame had been twisted out of shape by the bus's bumper. The lovely overhead bar on my sports car sat there, pathetically gnarled like a paperclip bent by a bored child.

I pushed upward on the roof panel, debris falling from my shoulders. I felt as if I were trapped under a pile of garbage. That's what my beloved car had turned into: a total wreck. It was fit for nothing more than the junkyard.

And what was left? Me. My life.

I was still struggling to comprehend what had happened. I felt pelts of wetness on my face and realized it was raining. The chill of the fall air and the dampness soaking through me urged me to think hard about what happened.

In my daze, I began to recall that a semi-truck loaded with gravel had been right behind me when I swerved into the ditch. Since the heavy load was heading toward my rear bumper at 50 mph, I instinctively knew I was in danger of having it smash me from behind.

Recalling this perilous situation, I panicked and pulled myself upright into the driver's seat. Gripping the steering wheel, I hauled myself up until I could stand up in the driver's seat.

Looking around at the debris, I knew I had been in a wreck. I saw that the T-top frame had been driven straight through the passenger seat. Thank God no one was sitting beside me!

Again, I remembered the gravel truck. Panicking, I jumped over the car's passenger door onto the pavement.

As I took in the surrounding scene, I realized that the bus was there, and the gravel truck had safely pulled to the side of the road. The semi was not heading my way. I sighed a breath of relief.

"Are you okay?" People were running toward me, expressions of disbelief lining their faces.

I told them I was fine. Just a bleeding bump on my forehead. No big deal.

"Are you sure you're, okay?" Strangers asked me in amazement. I almost cried when I saw you push things off yourself and stand up in the driver's seat. I was at the intersection, waiting to cross the highway, and I saw the entire accident." I looked toward where he pointed, trying to grasp the details of his story. "Your car went under the rear right corner of the bus, and I saw the top of your car get cut half off! I immediately thought that you were decapitated!" I blinked in wonder, trying to comprehend the meaning of what just happened. "It's a miracle you are still alive and standing here. I'm so grateful and happy."

A Miracle

He spelled it out for me. It was a miracle. I was still alive. I was standing here. He was grateful and happy. But was I? I was still too stunned to know.

Other people were standing around, talking, inspecting everything that had happened. Though it was only a few minutes, it seemed like I had been at that scene for hours. I felt like I was standing there, like a cameraman, panning around the area and watching the scene unfold.

Just then, a policeman appeared and approached me. "Where's the body of the man who was driving the Corvette?" I told him I had been driving it. He stared at me, dumbfounded. "Are you kidding me?" He nearly laughed, thinking I must be joking. "You were in that car and walked away?" Still dazed, I answered that I didn't walk far, just a few steps. He chuckled, incredulous. "Your head is bleeding. You should go to the hospital."

Realizing I was not the only one in the accident, I asked if all the children in the bus were okay. The police officer assured me that they were all alright. Just a few bumps and bruises.

The ambulance eventually arrived and took me to the hospital. The staff examined me, bandaged my wounds, and later released me to go home.

To this day, I don't understand how I walked away unhurt. Clearly, God had worked a miracle in preventing my death. He must have had plans for me. What was He calling me to do?

He had given me another chance at life.

Chapter 2: No Need for a Name

Most kids can't wait to grow up. As children, we believe that once we reach adult status, we will finally be free. Free to do what we want when we want.

No one will rush us out the door for school, remind us to eat our vegetables, scold us for walking in the house with muddy shoes, or give us a stern look when we want to stay up late. We will be able to make our own decisions according to our own principles.

Once I broke free from my parents' house, I slowly realized that adulthood wasn't the freedom I had envisioned. Those childhood experiences continue to influence and shape my fears and desires.

If you take a good hard look at your life, you might realize that many of your decisions— perhaps most of them, in fact—are made as reactions to what you grew up with. Your choices in life are either shunning past traumas or embracing those childhood values. So, it was with me.

My father was a man who always thought outside of the box. He often came up with forward-thinking ideas. I will always remember the idea he suggested I recommend to the 4H club.

The club had asked each student to develop an idea to benefit our community. We lived in rural Wisconsin farm country. Although it was the middle of the 20th century, many families in the area had no TV and no indoor toilet. Most people today consider both of those necessities. For my time and area, they were rare luxuries.

No one who has ever had to do it once would easily forget running to an outhouse during the winter when temperatures were dipping 20°F below zero. I had to do it every winter until I was high school age!

The local farms were scattered away from each other. Still, everyone knew every owner of every farm around. Knowing your neighbors was how you identified everyone's address.

When asked where a particular family lived, the answer would be something like this: "They live right next to the Smith farm." Of course, anyone needing to ask for directions to find a particular family probably wouldn't be familiar with where the Smith farm was either.

You couldn't direct a visitor to "turn left on Main Street" or "follow River Road for a couple miles" because, in my community, the streets had no names. The farms had no street addresses. All addresses were Rural Route One. The postman knew everyone on his mail route. There was no need for it since we all knew each other and where we all lived. Everything was country roads, and you navigated by various landmarks to get where you wanted to go.

Therefore, directions to a place might sound like this: "You go past the Harley farm, continue straight, past two gravel roads, then go right at the second road. Go down that road aways and you should see a red schoolhouse." They were referring to a one-room school back then, not some multi-story complex on five acres like we see today. The directions would continue: "At the schoolhouse, go left and follow that road about two miles and you'll find the place that you're looking for." It was as simple as that.

Of course, it wouldn't be so simple if you hadn't grown up in the community and learned these things from the time you were a kid. Outsiders might wonder how an ambulance or fire truck would find the right place in an emergency. For us, it was easy. Everyone knew where everyone lived, so it was no problem.

Regardless, my father said I should recommend that each farm and building on the roads have a unique number posted on a standard red sign with reflective letters. That way, emergency vehicles could easily find the location of the emergency. Emergencies in those days frequently involved barns catching on fire. Naturally, emergency workers often relied on their senses, eyeing the smoke or flames until they eventually reached the fire. But still, wouldn't it be nice to have an address for where you need to be?

I liked my father's idea and proudly went off to the 4H club meeting feeling that I would undoubtedly have the best recommendation.

When my turn arrived, I confidently stood and presented the idea: an easy solution to help the community in emergency situations. Much to my surprise, the idea was met with raucous laughter. "Are you an idiot? Everyone knows the name of every farm. What a dumb idea. Sit down." My eager anticipation of praise swiftly shifted to an urgent desire to disappear. Heat rose in my face as I returned to my chair. I never thought I'd be ridiculed for offering to move the community into modern times.

I vowed right then and there to one day leave this stagnant town. I'd move to a place where people appreciated progressive ideas. I'd find a group of people who wouldn't dream of mocking me. When I finally got out of this place, no one would tell me to sit down.

My Father's Guidance

My father looked at my options for what I might do after high school. He suggested that I study computers since they were the wave of the future, and he knew I was good with electronics. He recognized that I wouldn't be happy carrying on his school bus business. A computer programming career offered success and fulfillment.

Yet would that form of success really make me happy. I wasn't so sure.

The Call of My Youth

A quiet inner voice had spoken to me in my youth. God had been trying to get my attention. That gentle guidance — perhaps you recognize it as your conscience, your guardian angel, or God Himself — leads you to take certain paths rather than others. Whenever you encounter a fork in the road and must choose between two paths, you stop and listen interiorly for advice on which is the better path to take.

I recall first experiencing that inner voice as a calling. I was around the age of reason, about six or seven years old. I felt God nudging me to consider going into the Ministry.

This was a serious matter. I didn't know how I felt about it at the time. I looked at my own pastor and wondered if I could really be like him. I wondered if I wanted to be.

My parents had raised me in a Christian home. Without fail, they brought my brothers and me to church every Sunday. Church always felt like a safe place, a sanctuary. For the most part, I felt welcome and at peace there.

However, like most kids, patience ran short when having to sit quietly in the pew for an hour. The wood benches were uncomfortable, and the whole routine of sitting, standing, listening, and reflecting did not seem to accommodate children's short attention spans and cravings for entertainment. Often, my brothers and I would get restless and start horsing around.

My father's stern stare in our direction sufficed to stop our antics. One look from him, and we knew we would "get it" once the service ended.

My father avoided embarrassing the family or causing a disruption in church. So, he would wait until we had driven beyond the sight of the church crowds before pulling off the road to reprimand my brothers and me.

I sometimes wonder if my father intentionally waited until after service ended as a way to draw out our anxiety over the impending punishment which awaited us!

Our church did offer Sunday School before service. We learned some key lessons about God and His Word. However, the energy we got from spending time with our peers didn't help much once the fun ended and church service began.

We kids developed a view of church service as a torture test, relief coming only during a few church songs.

Our pastor did not exactly exude the joy of the faith. His staunch seriousness made us kids wish to avoid him as much as possible.

The Pastor's Glare

One Sunday, he ceased his sermon mid-sentence! We all looked around, wondering what was wrong. Did someone faint? Was there a fire? What on earth would interrupt the pastor from his sermon?

His glare fell upon several kids who had been acting up. The congregation became utterly silent and on edge. The targeted children suddenly realized all eyes—particularly the pastor's peeved ones—were on them. They stopped. He started again. But the mood was one of dread until the service ended.

Typically, the pastor would stride to the rear church exit to greet church members. This Sunday, however, the pastor bolted down the church aisle like a professional football player heading for the touchdown line. Rather than play defense and try to block him, the disruptive boys fled, knowing full well he was after them. The pastor snatched them by the shoulders, stopping them in their tracks. For a split second, I thought he might tackle them to the ground! I was glad I was not among them.

You might be wondering whether the parents stepped in to defend their wayward children from corporal punishment. In those days, it was perfectly acceptable – even welcome – to have nonparental authority figures like pastors and teachers swat kids for being disrespectful or causing disruption. Everyone understood that such reprimands were part of one's duty to the community.

The memory of that moment stuck with me my entire life. Religion was serious business calling for serious action. I didn't know if I could be strict enough to command such compliance.

We were reminded that day that God was not happy with goofy behavior. A wave of guilt set in over our tendencies toward childishness. I could practically hear God admonishing me: *Why did you not listen when Pastor was speaking to you about My Word?*

As a child, God's voice seemed as if it came from a disappointed father whose satisfaction derived primarily from my guilt over not making better choices or being a better person.

As I grew older, I did less horsing around and became pensive about God. Sometimes people would comment that I was a very serious young man and should consider being a minister. I cringed at such suggestions. If being serious meant I was fit to be a pastor, then I needed to lighten up. When I imagined speaking at the pulpit in church each Sunday, I envisioned a dreary life of reminding people what they should and should not do. In other words, not much fun at all.

I wanted more out of life. I wanted to experience other cultures. I wanted to see how people lived in other areas, other states, other countries even! I wanted to witness what motivated people. Did everyone search for God in their own way? I felt there were answers out there, beyond my small, confined Wisconsin community, waiting to one day reveal themselves to me.

I wanted to discover them all.

Chapter 3: Back on the Old Track

We all experience moments when we view the bigger picture and realize that our life is not exactly on the right path. Perhaps this revelation comes to us during a vacation, a spiritual retreat, or after the sudden death of a loved one. Certain circumstances force us to stop our frenzied routine and step back for a moment to reassess where we are going and what changes should be made.

These times are moments of grace. We can humble ourselves enough to admit that things have been a little out-of-whack. We can resolve to do better. Be more committed to our family. Reconnect with old friends. Make time for spiritual and creative projects that rejuvenate us. We can know deep in our soul that all those little efforts would make us a better version of ourselves.

And yet, when it comes time to do it, we find that old habits are indeed hard to change. We might do well for a while, but gradually, without clear goals and support, we veer into the same old rut that left us stranded and weary in the first place.

That's how it was with me after my run-in with the school bus.

As soon as the insurance money came in from my totaled Corvette, I instantly saw it as an opportunity to buy a new one! You better believe I tested the brakes this time when taking it out for a drive!

I'll be more cautious this time, I told myself. What happened to me was a rare occurrence, and like a lightning strike, I trusted I'd never have to suffer through that twice.

Don't get me wrong. I was grateful for a brief period. I promised myself I would become a better person and try to answer God's calling. But that was short-lived.

When I looked back on my calling from God, I just wasn't convinced I'd be a good fit for going into ministry.

Seminary Visit

As previously mentioned, I felt God's call early in life to minister to His people. That invitation remained at the back of my mind all throughout my school years.

Attending parochial school supported my parents' emphasis on being God-conscious. I knew God was important, even if I wasn't always sure exactly how to place Him first in my life. Or even if I wanted to center my life around Him.

When I was about twelve, the school arranged a field trip for boys in my class to visit a seminary to learn more about the ministry. We stayed a few days with the college students. I wondered if this trip might solidify God's call in my life. Perhaps I would notice something that would make the ministry seem interesting. Perhaps it wasn't as serious and no-frills as my pastor had made it out to be. I had an open mind going into the trip.

When we first met the college seminarians, they were upright, serious students. That was what I had anticipated, and I felt like maybe I could be one of them when I got older. After all, people were always commenting on how serious I was. As the day wore on, however, their attitude began to change. I guess the seminarians initially felt a duty to be on their best behavior for us kids. But once they got more comfortable, their behavior slipped more and more into party mode.

It turned out that they were little better than any regular college students. Once the sun went down, these guys got out the beer, cigarettes, playing cards, and gambling money! I couldn't believe my eyes! Everything I had thought about the strict sheltered life of ministry (or at least seminarians studying for ministry) crumbled to pieces.

Back at my bunk, I tried to process this carousing side of life that I had never considered before. It occurred to me that I had never seen much of my pastor outside of church. Did he too puff cigarettes and guzzle beer when away from the pulpit? It was hard to imagine. But I really didn't know. At age twelve, it seemed there was a lot to learn about how people portrayed themselves versus how they were when no one was looking.

Were most people leading a double life? Was such duplicity reserved for people going into ministry? Would I be expected to put on a holy face in God's house but then return to my house to indulge in a decadent lifestyle? I didn't know if I could live like that.

I ruminated over the experience. Surprisingly, I found myself drawn toward being serious once again. As I contemplated my future life, I began to think more about my seminary experience. I dismissed the nighttime pleasures and found myself interested in reading and studying the Bible. What did God really want to tell us? What was His ministry all about? I became interested in bringing souls to Christ. That mission—the mission of every devout Christian—became prominent in my young mind.

As the days passed, my faith continued to grow, and I began to hear God's voice telling me I should become a minister. I decided to go into a career in ministry.

I had been "called." I intended to follow that call.

Heeding the Call

Certain of my future, I eagerly told my mother about my decision.

"Are you sure about that?" she asked. It's not that she wasn't thrilled to have a son thinking about entering the ministry. She just wanted me to not rush into anything. She continued, "You're very young to be making those kinds of decisions. You have time to think about it, so give it some time."

I thought the ministry over for the next few weeks. I mostly thought about what I would miss out on rather than the fulfillment I would gain through answering God's call. I wondered if anyone would want to date or marry me once I became a minister. I wondered if I'd ever be able to do fun things or have meaningful friends. I thought about my own minister, who seemed to live a life where his only time to get out was on Sundays when he sternly addressed the church and reprimanded kids for not listening to his sermon. Finally, I questioned what kind of financial means ministers had. My own family just scraped by, so I imagined it was even tougher for ministers to survive. Most likely, I would not be able to get a boat or a snowmobile like I had always dreamed of buying once I grew up. That's when I really started waffling on my decision to go into the ministry.

Perhaps God didn't know how much a boat would make me happy. Perhaps He underestimated how badly I wanted a snowmobile. God wants all of us to be happy, right? If that were indeed true, then it seemed to me and my middle-school mind that the ministry was not the career for me.

Of course, once I found my money-making career, I would certainly hand off a portion of that money to God's people. I would be ministering to them in a roundabout way, wouldn't I? That's how I rationalized my desire for wealth.

That reasoning stayed with me throughout high school and college and as I started my marketing career. The problem was that even though I made a lot of money, it never seemed that I made enough to be able to share it. Boats and snowmobiles cost a lot to pay for and keep up. If I sacrificed some of my wealth to share with the needy folks, I would be sacrificing some of my own happiness. And I wasn't ready to do that. No matter how much I got, no matter how much I had, I wasn't ever ready to give to others.

After my dire car accident, I was grateful to be alive. I thought there must be a reason God worked a miracle for me, and I thought about maybe doing things differently. Focusing more on people and less on things.

But soon, I was back in the driver's seat of another sporty Corvette. Yes, I was on the road again. Following the same old path, chasing after material possessions.

Chapter 4: A Shared Love

At this point, you might be thinking I was a selfish jerk, the kind you might like to glare at when you meet up with him at the stoplight. I admit I could be a jerk at times, but I was basically a good person.

I understood that success came through dedication and hard work. I had learned the lesson that God helped those who helped themselves. I had respected and honored my father and my mother. I cared for and looked after my twin brothers, who came along a couple years after me. And once I got to college, I learned to truly love another person.

Two Loves

After high school, I worked for a couple years loading trucks. That got old fast, mostly because I wasn't making the money I wanted.

My father knew I had always sought after something lucrative. He also knew I had a mind for technology. So, he suggested I study computers, as they were the wave of the future. I always respected my dad's keen awareness of rising progress, and I agreed with his assessment of what was flooding the market at that time. I had no doubt I could become rich in that business. I loved the idea of working in an office, firing up the huge mainframe computer, and writing in some coded language that only a special minority of the population at the time truly grasped or understood. The only glitch was that I hated programming!

I got by alright in my classes, learning some Cobol and Fortran, ancient computer languages. But the precise, step-by-step detail component was just killing me. I was horrible at math, and often Computer Science majors minor in math. Other students in my class were loving every minute of it. I just loved the idea of where it could get me.

Needless, I soon lost interest and pursued another 'career path': snowmobiling. I would ride around most of the night and sleep off the day. I also worked shifts loading trucks for a big beverage company, so, of course, my grades suffered. Ultimately, I dropped out of school. I knew snowmobiling didn't pay, and loading trucks allowed me to live paycheck to paycheck, but I wanted more than that.

I began looking for something that would make me some dough and make me want to get out of bed each morning. A coworker happened to hand me his college course catalog, and I noticed a new field I had never heard of before: Marketing.

The attraction was instant. I could not believe how exciting it sounded. I knew I would have to pay my own way. Still, I also knew my dedication and hard work would cover any financial obligations necessary for my education.

Pursuing the Dream

I dove into my classes mid-year and quickly surmised that I was indeed in the right field. I loved my classes. I loved being on campus. I loved...that girl on the 7th floor of the women's dorm who would sometimes stand in the window.

I knew my roommate was dating a girl in that dorm on that floor, so I asked if he knew who she was. "I know who she is," he said. "You'd like her. She drives a Mustang just like yours." From that moment on, I knew it was meant to be.

I couldn't contain my joy. I called out her name, shouting that I loved her maroon Mustang and informing her that I had one too. (All the cool kids back then drove Mustangs. It was the hot car of the decade.) I was sort of creating a scene by shouting up to the 7th floor, so I invited her to come down to the dorm lobby so we could talk. She agreed, and we hit it off instantly.

It turned out we had more in common than just driving Mustangs. She was from Chicago but was familiar with Wisconsin from traveling to a resort her grandmother owned in the state's northern section. She knew my hometown from driving right through it on trips to see her grandma!

We soon started dating. What a catch I had found! I was determined to make myself worthy of such a wonderful young woman. I'd prove how great I could be.

Meanwhile, I was doing great in my marketing classes. Working to pay my college costs, I still managed to make the Dean's List! I studied diligently, eager to get my degree and get started in a job. It was a new field, so I wanted to be among the first ambitious applicants with marketing degrees.

My girlfriend and I were also having lots of fun and getting serious. Everything was going better than I could ever have imagined. I dedicated myself to my studies and my work I saw my whole life as a red carpet rolling out before me, and I was generally thrilled to face each day. My joy was contagious. We wanted to be with each other exclusively and I was totally happy with life.

My dreams for recognition, success, and happiness were coming true. But at the back of my mind, I had a nagging fear that maybe I didn't deserve all the accolades I was getting. Perhaps if people knew that I was just a Wisconsin boy from a farm town who never had much, they would think differently of me. The thought was like an ever-present weed that thrived whenever my success waned. When life got dark and cloudy, that nagging insecurity arose and strangled much of the good in my personality.

In college, though, life was a string of sunny days, and I felt that my future was very bright. I asked my girlfriend to marry me, and she agreed. We were both free spirits, and we wanted to enjoy life freely, together.

We married before my last year of college. She was already working for a major airline, and due to her airline benefits, we were able to travel together frequently. Experiencing new places together for the first time was an incredible thrill for both of us.

Life together proved to be new, exciting, and grand. We were in love with each other, and all that the world had to offer.

I completed my degree requirements in three and a half years instead of the usual four, proudly toting my bachelor's degree in marketing. I knew I would get a great, well-paying job right away. And I did.

An insurance company hired me to get started in their marketing department. I poured myself into that company, working very hard to rise as quickly as possible. The company's management group soon recognized my dedication and boosted me up the corporate ladder.

I soon learned that I was making more money than most people my age. I was back on track to making my fortune. Back on track to fulfilling my dream toward financially driven happiness.

Chapter 5: Unsuitable

There are certain childhood moments that you recall vividly because they have come to define you. The way you thought as a child in that circumstance solidified your outlook on life. It didn't matter if it wasn't exactly true or didn't make a whole lot of sense. You considered it fact, given the evidence you had at the time. You never took the time once you got older to understand that maybe you weren't correct about everything in how you perceived the situation.

That's how it was with me and my self-image. From the time I was very young, I felt inferior to my peers. This was most evident to me in my appearance, which stood out to me even more once I moved beyond my small farming community friends and entered the wider world of high school.

My parents never had much money to purchase a whole new wardrobe for me every school year as I grew out of my clothes. Back-to-school shopping for me meant I would receive one new pair of pants and two new shirts. I was the oldest, so at least I didn't have to wear hand-me-downs like my younger brothers did.

Since I had to make a pair of pants and a couple of shirts last all year long, my parents bought clothes for me that were very practical and durable. They were never fashionable or fancy. Stylish clothes were considered "Sunday clothes". Our Sunday best was reserved for church or other special occasions.

Bravo!

One such special occasion arose when my school scheduled a field trip to watch a youth play in a church in the city, about 50 miles away. On the day of the play, my mother drove me to school to join the other kids. Some of my good school friends would be in the play, so I was very excited about going with them to this event. I was excited until I realized that I wasn't at all dressed nice enough to attend a play. I wasn't even dressed nice enough to go into a church.

What had my mom been thinking, sending me to a special occasion in plain school clothes? Surely, she wouldn't want me to go to such a grand event dressed as I would for any regular day.

The other boys were wearing suits or sport coats and ties. I just had casual slacks and a polo shirt. No suit. No tie. No button-down shirt even.

None of my classmates said anything to me. But I knew they must be thinking it. I couldn't possibly be the only one thinking what a bum I was for not dressing up for such a special occasion. I was embarrassed. No, I was mortified. I couldn't possibly go like this. But I wanted to be there to see my friends. I wanted to clap for them and, in the end, give them a standing ovation. At the end of the play, I would stand tall in my nice suit, calling *Bravo!*

I couldn't call out *Bravo!* In slacks and a polo. I had to think of something quick. I jogged to my grandmother's house, ten blocks from school. My grandmother answered the door and looked at me with loving pity. She never scolded me for going to her house, even when she probably suspected I was frequently visiting her because I was playing hooky from school.

This day, she couldn't help me much since she didn't drive and had no car. She had a phone, though, so I could try to get someone else to help me. I frantically hooked my finger in the appropriate holes of the rotary dial phone, trying to get hold of any aunt or uncle who could come to my assistance. One by one, I explained my predicament: I needed someone to go to my parent's house, get my suit, bring it to me at my grandmother's house in town, then drive me fifty miles to the play so I could stand in my suit at the end and call out *Bravo!* Okay, I left out the part about what I'd do at the end of the play.

Each relative listened to my dire need and turned me down. I couldn't believe that they couldn't or wouldn't find the time to help me. The nicer ones didn't bother with listing all the things they had to do that day instead of chauffeuring me around. Instead, they patiently explained to me that by the time they went to my parent's house, then drove to my grandmother's house to pick me up, then took me to the play fifty miles away, the play would be over. It wasn't that they didn't want to (although they didn't say they really did want to); it was just that they couldn't. Unless I discovered a way to travel through time, my attendance at the play just wasn't going to happen.

By the time I had finished all my phone calls, there definitely was no way I could make it to the play on time. I slumped on my grandmother's couch, defeated. No play. No church. No clapping for my friends and calling, *Bravo!*

The next day at school, my friends asked me where I had gone. I told them I hadn't been feeling good and ended up going to my grandmother's house. It wasn't exactly a lie.

Sunday Best Every Day

When I reached adulthood and began working, I started buying my own wardrobe, I bought lots of suits. I learned that suits could be worn in many places besides church. I wore them to work, to meetings, to social events, and, yes, to church whenever I decided to go.

I was always good at finding suits and ties. My spouse was even better, so, thanks to her excellent taste, all my shirts, ties, and suits coordinated well. This served us well whenever we made an important appearance.

There were times when some company would be arriving in town, and we'd have to impress them. As a successful young businessman in Chicago, I soon learned where all the best fine-dining places were and frequented them. When the need arose, I would call the restaurant and speak to the maître d'. Each of them treated me like an old friend. Even the places that didn't have openings for months would say, "Mr. Lemke? Oh, yes, we will have a table for you and your guests this Saturday. It will be our pleasure to have you join us."

Nice suits felt grand. Name recognition felt amazing. Immediate table reservations in a restaurant with a months-long waiting list felt spectacular.

Chapter 6: Caging the Free Bird

The large insurance company that had hired me was a direct marketer that owned their own production facilities, including an advertising agency, plus printing, mailing, and data services. They promoted me to manage the data services business unit.

These "in-house" production businesses completed all the production for the insurance parent. They also sold their services to outside companies to offset the insurance company's costs. The insurance company then bought outside data and information through brokers. Meanwhile, the brokers made a twenty-percent commission for the data and info they provided.

Being young, ambitious, and full of ideas for success, I decided my data business could bring all that work and the brokerage commissions in-house which would save the insurance company millions of dollars. The company supported the idea when I pitched it to them. Glad to have the company's support, I formed a sales team, that provided services to the insurance company, also started selling to outside companies. This transitioned my team from overhead to a profit center We were a successful and profitable business, growing quickly.

Being a successful businessman required much entertaining of outside clients. I would go on extended "three-martini" lunches with potential clients I sought to win over. That's how you did business and built relationships with clients back then. You sat and chatted and spent time getting to know one another. Each person spent time assessing the other before delving into a business relationship with them. In those days, business relationships were more personal, more based on established trust.

Things are much more direct and to-the-point in today's business world. Each method has its benefits. People no longer sip three martinis during a business lunch—not even one or two! At least that altered aspect of doing business is probably a good thing.

While it was true that my hard work and innovative ideas got me the success I enjoyed, I admit that often I acted "too big for my britches." I started behaving like a big shot, thinking I was invincible. I became arrogant, cocky, and a veritable, first-class jerk.

My hunger for success became insatiable. I chased after the "little extra" assignments that were sure to pay off big dividends if I just pushed myself a bit harder. Often, I stayed after work or went for drinks with coworkers, while my wife sat home alone. Worse yet, sometimes I worked while she sat stranded at her work because I had commandeered her car and hadn't picked her up to take her home! I had become a self-centered control freak.

I just had this incessant urge to prove myself worthy of my success. No matter what my wife told me about how much she loved me for who I was and that I didn't need to seek after bigger and better positions, I had convinced myself that I had to be more. My wife came from Chicago's upper-end suburbs. Her father was a successful banker who had earned lots of money and provided his family with everything that they needed, including a large home with a pool, exotic vacations, and a nice lifestyle. Remember, his in-laws even owned a resort in Northern Wisconsin!

Even though I was still in my mid-twenties, for whatever reason, I felt I had to compete with my father-in-law's success and offer that level of luxury to my wife. She never asked me to be any more than who I was. Still, my deep-seated feelings of inferiority made me restless and resentful when I couldn't live up to being the person whom I felt she deserved.

Slump

The nagging pressure from my skewed self-image drove a wedge deeper and deeper into my marriage.

My early success caused a shift in my attitude and, ultimately, my whole personality. The more material possessions I gained, the bigger my ego became. My family and friends noticed the changes occurring before I ever did. I didn't know what they were so perturbed about. Why shouldn't I be proud of what I was accomplishing? I didn't acknowledge that the "big shot" lifestyle was transforming me, and not for the better.

I became even cockier and began thinking about how I could make more money. I always had an entrepreneurial attitude and saw that core trait as the way to make real money.

When the economy plummeted and the insurance company started laying off people, I panicked. I couldn't face the prospect of having the company place me on the chopping block. So, I decided to ensure my position with a savvy business deal. I convinced my sales guys to join me in buying the business from the insurance company. I explained to the fellas that we could pay for it by continuing to service the insurance company through the twenty percent commissions we earned from their work and we would also be free to build a complete outside client base, insuring that we would continue to increase our cash flow In some ways, that would be considered a leveraged buyout in today's world, but there was no business term for it back then.

We hired a financial consultant and a lawyer to put together an 'offer to buy' proposal so we could present it to the insurance company management for their consideration. We were all confident the insurance company would accept our proposal. In our cocky, arrogant young minds, there was no way they could possibly refuse.

They did.

Even worse, they viewed my sales partners and me as disloyal employees. My partners and I decided we would resign if they turned down the proposal. We knew they would never trust us again, so we turned in our papers and left.

We figured we could be plenty successful on our own. We didn't need the big guys at the insurance company anyway. Man were we wrong! Or at least I was.

We formed a company and went into business for ourselves. At first, we were flying high.

Self-employment meant working on a straight commission. All the dough went directly to us. No cuts to the big management bosses. That was all fine and dandy until I realized that I had belonged to the big management bosses!

I had made my money through the pool of funds that everyone contributed to after their sales. I had worked the role of directing everyone in their jobs. They, in turn, had shared their profits with me.

Starting a business for ourselves, each person was paid based on what we sold individually. My sales partners had clients. Once I took over the department as the group manager, I had not built those relationships with clients, so I had no clients and had to start completely from scratch.

Initially, I had been infatuated with freedom. The idea of breaking free of the large corporation and owning a private business had been intoxicating. It didn't occur to me just how long the sales cycle was from the time you make a sale until the time you get paid.

It wasn't long before I recognized with great dread and shame that I would not be bringing home any money for some time.

Ultimately, the lack of sales drained me financially.

We would have to be completely dependent on my wife's income. I felt embarrassed and foolish. Just seeing her each time, I came home reminded me how ridiculous I had been and how I didn't deserve her as a wife. My frustration with myself over my poor foresight led me to turn away from the very person who could have helped me get back on my feet. Rather than accept her loving help, I withdrew more and more from our relationship.

My insecurity made me depressed, irritable, and generally miserable to be around. All my actions led to the destruction of the relationship. I became a different man than the freedom-loving entrepreneur she had fallen in love with. She began to give me more space to work things out on my own. She tried to support me, but my constant rumination, moodiness, and refusal to do things together took its toll. I no longer laughed or smiled. I was generally a miserable person and miserable to be around.

We no longer had money to travel and do things we enjoyed together. I began to wonder if she had any reason to stay with me since I couldn't provide the enjoyments she wanted in life. I began to worry that my wife would leave me for someone more successful. Someone with more money who was more fun to be around. I became a jealous lunatic.

The cinch that strangled anything good we had left in our marriage was my efforts to control her. She and I had fallen in love under the pretext that we were both free spirits and would allow each other to live freely. Yet, when money matters loomed like a black cloud over our relationship, I became very suspicious, asking where she had gone and whom she had spent time with. I wanted to know her every move. I knew I was stifling her, yet I couldn't shake the feeling that if I could somehow control her, I would make her stay with me.

Naturally, the more control I exerted, the more she wanted to break free from my obsessiveness. I had proved myself right: she didn't want to be with a failure like me. She filed for divorce. Vindicated, knowing I had been right all along, I signed the papers.

In retrospect, my incessant insecurity combined with my drive to prove that I belonged among the wealthy had led me down the path to divorce. In the end, I sold my share of the company to my partners and sought another job.

PART II

Do you ever return home from your parents' house and wonder, "Man, when will I quit feeling like a child around them?"

Do you cringe when an old high school buddy says, "Wow, you really haven't changed!"?

Do you find yourself getting to the age — 30, 40, 50 — when you thought you'd finally have it all together, when you thought you'd have it made; then you find that you still feel like that insecure twelve-year-old, just in a weaker, stouter body? Nothing has really changed. You're still you. Still struggling. Still nursing the same old wounds.

That's how it was with me at the time....

Chapter 1: Please Tell Me

After the divorce, I didn't know what to do. I was still struggling financially, and my dissolved marriage didn't help my feelings of failure any. Not only had I disappointed myself, but I had also put a black mark on my family name. No one in my family history had divorced, ever!

You went through hard times with each other, and you stuck it out. That's just the way it was. You made your vows before God and kept your promises to each other. For better or worse, for richer or poorer. Period. No discussion.

The dissolution of my marriage was like a death in the family—like a shameful suicide—that no one dared talk about.

It seemed that for all the times I thought maybe I wasn't so bad after all; this act had finally had me cross over to the "bad" side. I knew my family was disappointed in me. I craved their understanding. I wanted to know they still loved me despite this seemingly unforgivable sin — letting my marriage fall apart.

One thing I missed about my wife was her loving family. They weren't very religious, but they were kind people, always expressing their love to one another. It blew my mind how casually they would say, "I love you" at the end of every conversation. The words just rolled out of their mouths like it was the most natural phrase in the world. My parents had never been like that. The word "love" was completely absent in our house. I didn't hear my parents say it to each other (although I'm sure they did) and they didn't say it to me and my brothers. You just took it for granted that they loved you. One day, the need to actually hear it really got under my skin. I decided to go visit my dad and ask him straight out. I hopped in my car and drove 5 hours to catch him working in the farm fields. "What are you doing here?" he asked, surprised that I would travel such a long way to show up without warning.

I told him I needed to know something. Never once had he told me that he loved me, and I just needed to know if he did or not.

My dad stood there, quiet. He had been caught off guard. Finally, he spoke. "My father never said those words to me either."

I stood a moment, dumbfounded at his response. Waiting for something more. Nothing more came. I got in my car and drove the five hours back home.

To be fair, my father might have had more to say if I had prepared him better. Perhaps if I had written him a letter and given him time to consider how to respond, maybe he would have weaved together some heartbreakingly beautiful prose that would have offered me the assurance I craved. Or perhaps if I had just stayed an hour or so, he would have had time to think it over and hear me out about why I needed to know I was loved.

In any case, he didn't answer, and I didn't stay. The hope I was looking for was not to be found with my father. I was on my own and would have to find answers elsewhere.

Although that was a painful moment in my life, I'm happy to report that many years later, I did get the answer I was looking for. While wheeling toward the surgery room for an operation on his heart, my father finally told my brothers and my mom and me that he loved us. Those were his last words, and ones I will carry in my heart always!

Eastbound

Eventually, I got a job out East and relocated there.

After a few years, I took different job, and that's where I met my second wife. She was a lovely, wonderful person some years younger than me. I started the job in November. In early December, we were both at the company Christmas party. There was a magical chemistry between us, and we spent the night dancing, talking, and laughing. The feelings between us were mutual and our romance began to blossom. Sometimes we would both be at a business lunch and would sit next to each other. We would secretly be holding hands under the table, making sure that we didn't get caught. Dating within the same company was considered a no-no, so we were discreet, but people just knew what was going on. I think the way we glowed around each other likely gave it away like a spotlight on a dark night.

The company opened an office in Chicago, and we were both transferred there. We had lots of fun enjoying the exciting things a large city like Chicago offers. Naturally, our relationship grew, and we decided to marry.

I was on top of the world. I had married a wonderful woman, moved up to number two guy in the office, driving a Porsche, buying a large boat, buying a huge house big enough so we could start a family. How could life be any better?

I'll tell you how. Simple. By getting more things. My flame of desire for success and fortune continued to glow even brighter. I set sights on my making great money, living in the huge new house, and making even more money.

I never really thought about the things I had as blessings from above. I was never really grateful. Nor did it occur to me to use my good fortune to help others. I figured it was my right to enjoy the fruits of my own labor.

With this self-centered outlook on life, I continued to keep my sights set on something bigger and better. *Maybe I should sell the Porsche and buy a Ferrari. Maybe we can put in a pool.* The bigger-and-better pursuits went on and on. Toys and more toys. Spend, spend, spend. From all appearances, I was a success. I continuously measured my success by the material things that I had. Appearances were everything. I had it made, and I was never again going back to being a poor boy from Wisconsin.

Success and Distress

Underneath all of that outside "success", there was an internal "distress." In addition to my craving for wealth, I was now driven by a terrible fear of losing everything. The incessant desire laced with the looming fear was a bad combination. Whenever my financial situation began to look low, I began to get neurotic.

In desperation to have success and keep it going at optimal levels, I spent much of my time working. The more I had, the more I wanted.

The fact that I bought luxury items and lived a grand lifestyle meant that I owned very little. The truth of the matter was that the bank owned most of it. I was merely making payments to appease them. The only things I had accumulated that were truly mine were lots and lots of debts.

Chapter 2: All the Little Wonders

I misspoke when I claimed that debt was the only thing that was truly mine. Something else came along that was more beautiful, more mesmerizing, more inspiring than any item I could have viewed in a store window: my kids.

Legacy

My wife and I were blessed with a baby boy. Then over the years, two girls came along as well. Wow! What could be better?

I was in the delivery room for each of their births. I remember the exact moment when they were delivered, cried, and began their life.

There is no earthly possession that one could ever acquire that's more valuable than a child. They were and still are God's greatest gift to me and I'm humbled and grateful beyond measure for each of them.

As I look back, I realize that I had absolutely no concept of what it means to be a father. The one word that comes to mind is responsibility. I'm now totally responsible for taking care of other human beings. What if I do something wrong? How do I set an example? What values do I need to instill in them?

The one thing that I wanted to instill in them was for them to know that they were loved. As unconditionally as I could possibly love them. After all, I had not heard that word in my childhood.

So, I made sure to tell them that I loved them every day. At one point, one of them said to me, "Dad, I know that you love me. You don't need to say it all the time." I said, "Yes, I do. I don't know that anyone can hear that they are loved too many times."

Beyond love, my wife and I both agreed that we wanted them to have a strong foundation in faith. We attended church as a family, and they all attended parochial grade school and high school. I hope that instilled in them that no matter what life brings, God is with you. If you trust Him, communicate with Him and just ask Him, He will guide you through whatever life dishes out.

They are each different and I love them for that. And I'm so proud of what each of them has done with their life. They've each accomplished things beyond my wildest expectations.

I believe that they are each following their hearts and doing what they really enjoy and going through life knowing that they are loved. I'm grateful to be a father and hope that I instilled the right things in them.

Digging Bigger Holes

Having a family of my own—a wife and three little ones—made me very proud. I knew they deserved all the best I could give them. I wanted to give them everything. Everything I never had. Everything I had wanted as a kid. Everything I thought other kids in the neighborhood had. I wanted them to have it all.

The more money I made, the bigger the debt I had. I was making the minimum payments just to keep the wheels of success spinning.

I understood the mound of debt was growing faster than my newborns were outgrowing their Carters outfits. But, what the heck? It was worth it, right? I kept buying things to ensure that my kids also felt they came from a successful home. It became a charade, and things were spinning out of control.

I told myself that I needed more income to comfortably support my growing family. I needed a larger and larger income to support my swiftly growing ego.

My success was so important to me that I hurt people, disappointed people, lied to people, and did countless other things which I am now ashamed of. How could I have gone this far off the road? People always told me that I was a nice guy. I regret that I lost that along the way. I lost my faith as well.

But I kept right on driving on that magic road of materialism. It seemed like every time I fell off the mountain and ended up in the valley, I would bounce back to an even higher mountain on the other side.

I was very blessed with the jobs that I had in my life, and it seemed like they always got better. Being a farm kid from Wisconsin, I went further than I could ever have imagined. My jobs took me to over thirty countries around the world. I met top businessmen, movie stars, athletes, race car drivers, musicians, politicians, and even an Arab sheik!

So Many Sights to See

I traveled from the Zen buildings of China to the vibrant countryside of Spain, from the reefs of Australia to the Alps of Switzerland, from the fantastic cliffs of New Zealand to majestic palaces of Germany, from the high-cultured streets of Great Britain to the rugged jungles of Brazil.

The list goes on. I saw places and things that most people only dream of viewing just once in a lifetime. And I loved it!

Zooming from continent to continent, I accumulated millions of reward air miles on multiple airlines. The only drawback was that I missed a great deal of time with my family.

So often, I would see something breathtaking. Although the experience thrilled me, it also caused me heartache because I wished I had my family at my side to experience it with me.

I missed my wife and kids, and I thought of them often. I convinced myself that all this time away was for their sake. To show them that I was thinking of them while away, I always brought home a souvenir of where I had traveled. I often wound up buying something at the airport because my business meetings generally didn't leave much time for thoughtful, considerate shopping.

I quickly developed a tradition of finding an item sold by virtually every airport gift shop in the world. Even in non-city stores, this item was often available, so it took little effort on my part. At the end of my flying days, my family had accumulated an enormous bowlful of these trinkets that I regularly purchased as travel gifts.

What were they? Souvenir key chains from wherever traveled to!

However, when I had the opportunity, I did purchase other items as well that were rarer and more unique: Snow globes, baseball hats, Chinese silk pajamas, genuine pearl necklaces from Hong Kong, beautiful silk scarves from India, serapes from Mexico, autographed celebrity photos, art objects, "lucky" crystal rocks, and of course, plenty of stuffed animals.

I don't remember the rest. And my family probably doesn't remember either.

When it was all said and done, I realized the one thing I hadn't bothered to spend on my family was the thing that couldn't be bought: time. All that my kids really wanted was time with me. They wanted me to know them! They wanted me to know their interests and friends and how they liked spending a lazy Sunday afternoon. They wanted me to love them not by spending my money on travel trinkets or even exotic gifts but by spending my time with them. It is summed up by my daughter on a hand drawn "greeting card" On the outside of the card it said, "Welcome Home Daddy. On the inside it said, "Daddy, your home! I missed you. Why did you have to go away for a week? Did you have to leave? I missed you. I love you!"

I still have that card in my desk and my eyes still water up when I read it.

Chapter 3: Where I Belong

Looking back, I realized that buying souvenirs was about three things: flaunting my success, showing how I had encountered different cultures from around the word, and making up for the guilt of being away from family.

Visiting Home

All of that traveling to various countries made me feel successful and important. I loved advancing to the head of the line before all the inexperienced travelers. At the airlines, I had earned VIP status. I didn't fly in coach for some twenty years. For a while, I was flying from Michigan to London every other week. Another time, I flew home to Michigan from Paris for the weekend—talk about insanity!

What people didn't see was how exhausting it all was. And, how lonely. So many times, when I was in some strange new place, I wished that my family could have been there with me. I showed them pictures and brought key chains and other souvenirs back to them, but the only memories of those places are only in my own mind. And I knew inside that I was not terribly important. The more accurate story was that I was a husband and father who was away from his family a whole lot.

My wife and kids created their own memories from doing school and dance, attending activities, and hanging out with friends. Sadly, those memories didn't include me. And the recollection of those times together didn't exist in my mind.

When we'd all finally be together again, my wife and kids weren't used to having me around. In fact, they had grown used to *not* having me around. Their daily routine didn't include me. The household operated just fine without my presence and without my input. Whenever the kids would say, "Hey remember that time when we all...." I couldn't share in the memory. I hadn't been there. I had become like a visitor in my own home.

Many People, Few Differences

Traveling enabled me to learn a lot about people and cultures. As a marketing person, I continuously sought to understand what leads people to purchase this versus that product or service. Essentially, I was a student of what motivates people's purchasing decisions. I knew that if I understood what concerned them, I could sell them products that they wanted to buy. Of course, I concerned myself with what people *wanted*, not necessarily what they needed.

I learned a great deal about people around the world. First, we are all God's creation. Thank God that He did make us all different! Why would anyone want to live in a world where everyone is the same? I don't know about you, but I would be bored to death, even if everyone was just like me.

Being different is exciting! We need each other's talents and insights to help us better navigate life's challenges. Individuals have different views of the same problem. But also, cultures carry their own strengths. The diligent meticulousness of the Germans balances the artsy splendor of the French. I found numerous, astounding differences in people and cultures wherever I traveled. I also found surprising basic similarities.

No Distance Too Far

One thing I did really care about more than growing my success and gaining material things was being there for my kids, as often as I could. I certainly wasn't the perfect dad. But I love them tremendously, and I tried to learn my lesson about being there for them when they needed me.

I felt guilty about all my traveling and not being at home. This guilt struck me hard when one year I missed my older daughter's birthday because of a business meeting on the West Coast set up a meeting and told me that I absolutely had to be there.

We met with a movie star at her house in Hollywood. She was a delightful and graceful hostess and personally served us coffee and cookies. While I was admittedly enthralled with being in the company of a famous person, the person I most wanted to be with was my daughter on her birthday.

My daughter was very gracious and understanding. But guilt still haunts me for missing that special day of my "star" and I'm very proud of her. Besides, not long after, I moved on to a different company. While it's only one day, it's a day that I can't get back and a lesson about priorities.

I did learn a lesson from some of my experiences. My younger daughter loved dancing and became quite a ballerina. She attended dancing schools and successfully competed all over the country. She won loads of trophies and awards throughout the years. I was incredibly proud of her and tried to attend as many of her recitals as I could. Of course, business travel often prevented me from attending some of her performances. Still, I always made a special effort to attend her final performance each year. This grand finale was a competitive event with other dance troupes, and I wanted to be there to witness all the progress she had made and to support her.

One year, my daughter's final recital required me to fly from Australia to Florida where she was performing. My sweet girl called me specifically to tell me not to worry about it. "Dad, you don't have to come all the way over here just to see me dance," she said. I had not been to any of her performances all season. I wanted to see her so bad. I knew that if I missed out on this, even though she said it would be okay, I would always regret it. I told her that it was worth flying halfway around the world to be with her for her special night.

I flew to the US, watched her perform, stayed overnight, then flew back to Australia the next morning. Other than pilots, I'm not sure anyone else has done an Australia to Florida and back turnaround trip. I spent more time in the air each way than on the ground for that visit. Yet, I was there for my daughter during her final recital.

Most people have told me I was crazy to do such a thing. I say putting my "star" daughter first made that visit the most worthwhile trip I've ever taken.

I also learned other lessons. There were times when I didn't properly support or defend my kids the way I should have. I remember not standing up for my son in a situation when I should have. I stuck up for other people which was wrong, and I know that I hurt him.

Thankfully, he is a strong leader and a "star" who always stands up for people and what is right. I'm very proud of him. He taught me a very important lesson.

As a parent, I've learned a lot from my kids, my greatest gift from God, and I trust that I was a good father, even with my mistakes.

Chapter 4: Many Facets of Life

Admittedly, traveling to so many various places taught me a lot about other people. It also taught me a lot about myself.

Something Bigger

I encountered rich people in mansions and poor people in their "blue tarp" hovel homes. I witnessed wealthy people soaking in Jacuzzis while another person served them cocktails. I observed poor people bathing while another person hand-pumped water into a bucket to pour over the naked streetside bather.

I had always believed that wealth equated to happiness or at least security. Interestingly, however, I met unhappy rich people who complained every day as well as "blue tarp" people (with no electricity, cell phone, or TV) sitting around a trash barrel fire while laughing and just enjoying life.

I viewed churches of many different faiths: Christianity, Judaism, Muslimism, Buddhism, and more. I also saw countries with essentially no religion, as the government had confiscated it from the people. Even in these societies and cultures, there is a sense of people seeking something beyond their physical lives.

I was fascinated by all the cultural and personal differences: food, dress, sports, housing, community, government, education, and entertainment.

Beyond Barriers

In every country I traveled to, I would always ask to try some of their local dishes. People of every region are always proud to show off their local dishes. Delicious food offered with a delightful presentation is the way we overcome our language barriers. Placing a good meal before a guest is a way to show hospitality. The appreciation for that excellent meal is a way to show gratitude.

I ate beef, chicken, fish, lamb, and pork, depending on the local customs and availability. The way these "standard" foods are prepared locally is astounding. There is virtually a smorgasbord of recipes, flavoring, and spices that create a nearly limitless variety of cuisine. They were all profoundly enjoyable.

I also ate some more exotic foods that you may not have tried: snake, goat, "skippy" (Australia slang for kangaroo), fish heads, grasshoppers, Peking duck, and other dishes that I was never quite sure what they were.

Hot and Cold

When traveling from country to country, continent to continent, I had to prepare for the variations in weather. The geographies and climates varied from extreme heat or cold, to deserts or mountains, oceans, and lakes.

The populations varied from sparse to overcrowded.

Some places felt almost claustrophobic, with billions of people bustling about their daily lives as best they could. For example, I once saw a family of five packed onto a moped, the baby seated on the handlebars while the vehicle weaved through traffic, with blue smoke billowing from the exhaust pipe of a dying engine.

Another time, I caught a man briskly walking down the highway at midnight while balancing bamboo branches on his head, rushing to who knows where. I saw people in third-world countries, sleeping in the median of a freeway.

Once, I saw an old woman, probably 80 years old, painting curbs in China. That was how she earned money to survive. Just painting her half-mile of curb yellow on both sides of the road. Then starting over again. No end, ever.

At the opposite end of the spectrum, I saw people relaxing around the pool at a 5-star hotel, doing absolutely nothing. These same folks would ride through town in limousines, attending social events with free-flowing champagne and caviar.

What fascinated me most about the various places I visited was always the people. While the cultures are all different, the people are much the same. Ultimately, they wanted a reasonable life filled with faith, freedom, family, work, security, fun, and enjoyment. Most of all, they wanted to love and be loved.

Regardless of the people or culture, emotional security — not material security — is ultimately the most valuable.

Chapter 5: Everything to Lose

I was not wealthy compared to many people; however, I was driven to become rich. While I realized that I had more material things than many other people did, it was still not enough. I always wanted more. And I kept trying to get more. The more that I had, the more "successful" I felt.

Meeting Milestones

No matter how many milestones I crossed, I continually carried with me an inner feeling of insecurity. I believed that if I accumulated enough material wealth, I would attain security. If I could get to a place where I finally had enough, I would never have to worry about being without again.

In my most successful year, I made over a million and a half dollars. *This is it! I* thought. *I'm a millionaire! I'm going to be living high! I'll be rubbing elbows with the big wigs!*

You would think it would have been the greatest day of my life. The pinnacle of my career. The moment when all my dreams came true! I should have been elated!

Instead, I was terrified: *What if I lose it all?*

It's important to understand that with every luxury item purchase, there was an added element of fear. I had to buy insurance on the items and take measures to secure them properly against theft. With every new item I owned, there was something new to worry about having taken away.

In my perfect dream life, everything would be paid for. I wouldn't owe anyone anything. I would have no more debt, so my "riches" could never be taken from me. With this dream in mind, I hoarded many of my material things, refusing to sell anything I had accumulated. At one point, I was paying for three rented storage units to store my toys, cars, snowmobiles, and other possessions.

I had not looked at or used many of these possessions for years or even decades. But I stubbornly held onto them. No one could take them from me! I was like a dragon jealously guarding his gold and gems. These items were mine. They were paid for and added to my so-called fortune. It didn't matter to me that the storage costs alone far outweighed the value of these treasures. I had moved them from state to state, keeping them with me as I relocated around the country. I owned them, and they had value to me. My rationale was that if I were ever again in a financial bind, I could sell these items, and they'd prevent me from being totally broke. Junk is junk and of no value to anyone.

My feelings of inferiority and the fear of losing all my possessions made me very nervous. I would sit at board meetings and eye all the people at the table. They all held advanced degrees from excellent schools. Sure, I had a bachelor's, but my 3 ½ years of study was nothing compared to the level of education these folks had.

Lesser Degree

Back when I attended high school, completing twelve years of primary education was a big deal. Farm kids who tired of the "3 Rs" — reading, writing, and arithmetic — could easily quit school under the guise of needing to help the family farm. I don't doubt some of those families legitimately needed the help of their young adults to keep the family farm going. However, once a student left high school, they rarely returned to complete their education.

Most kids who did graduate immediately began working. The determined minority pursued further education in college. In my house, no one discussed the possibility of advanced education. The expense prohibited my family and me from even considering it as an option.

I was able to put myself through college, and, as mentioned, I worked hard in my studies. But I always feared that if any of those other board members were to discover that I had never gone to an Ivy League school, they would laugh me out of the room.

I guess I should have given myself more credit. After all, I was there despite my lack of advanced education. That probably meant I had a good intuition about marketing which a person couldn't exactly get from school. But rather than pat myself on the back, I feared I had to watch my back instead, feeling like I would inevitably be first on the chopping block if ever the company had to lay people off.

Chapter 6: Life's Ups and Downs

I quelled my insecurity by accumulating more and more "wealth." I figured that if I amassed enough of it, I'd be comfortable for the rest of my life.

Hopefully, I could eventually make my children materially comfortable as well. And once they were comfortable and secure, then I could think about finally giving some of my riches back to God. I dreamt of fantastic fortunes gained by starting and selling businesses for millions. I dreamt of winning the lottery. I had a lot of other financial fantasies throughout my life, but I never attained them.

Crash and Burn

God had a different plan for me. As I continued down the road of materialism, I was learning that the "fun of owning" these things wore off as time went on. Nevertheless, the payments sure didn't.

Rather than wealth bringing me financial freedom, I quickly became a slave to the banks. With the high-interest rates, the alluring ability to pay the credit card debt off by making the minimum payment is like attempting to swim upstream. You can keep swimming and swimming and make no progress against the waves.

At some point, you realize that it is a futile effort, and you are forced to give up. You drown in debt.

That's what happened to me. When the economy crashed, I drowned in the sea of credit. I went bankrupt. I sank straight to the bottom, with only myself to blame. I lost everything I had owned. I discovered how ugly and brutal the bankruptcy process really is. No excuses. No emotion. Nothing personal, just business. Why should they accept any of my excuses? I was the one who got myself into the financial mess. They were going to make me pay up. Or take everything.

I couldn't pay. So, I lost it all.

There is an Old Testament saying that "There is desirable treasure, and oil in the dwelling of the wise, but a foolish man squanders it" (Proverbs 21:20). In today's terms: "A fool and his money are soon parted." Being forced to declare financial bankruptcy was like being hit over the head with a two-by-four.

It was a knock-down. It was also a wake-up.

God decided to take all my material treasures from me so I could have a chance to finally notice what really mattered.

I crashed and burned.

Another Crash and Burn

Crashing and burning by oneself is one thing. But there is always collateral damage. A person can't really love two things at once. You lose focus. That's what I did. My eyes were on the financial prize, not on the relationship prize. Something had to give.

After thirty-three years together, my second marriage collapsed. Things had been slipping for some time. But, being a fool, I had taken our marriage for granted. I returned to my old workaholic habits. I worked late. I worked weekends. I worked nights. Sometimes, I even worked on holidays. I rationalized this behavior as "doing it for the family." In retrospect, it was a lame excuse for me to again do what I thought was most important: to make money, to stay afloat, to preserve the façade.

I made many dumb decisions affecting my finances, which also affected my family. "Living large" put a heavy burden on my wife and me. Sometimes, decisions were made for me. For example, one time I unexpectantly lost my job. Losing that paycheck put me into a difficult financial situation very quickly. The months pass very quickly when you have no paycheck while the bills keep coming in.

Already stretched financially, I was stretched emotionally to the limits. My kids were small, and I had no money for Christmas presents. One of my best friends lent me his credit card and told me to go and buy some gifts for my kids and wife. That same year, I went outside on Christmas morning, and there by the garage door was a very large bag of presents for the kids. It ended up being one of the best Christmases they ever had, and it wasn't from any of my doing. To this day, I'm not sure who left those presents, but I will always be grateful for beloved friends.

Although I kept getting extraordinary signs that I didn't need to rely on my own strength, I struggled with all my might to get back what I had lost. I couldn't live with my failure. I couldn't face my family and friends after having lost everything.

I spent an inordinate amount of time on weekends juggling the finances and trying to keep the balls in the air. I'd be emotionally depressed all weekend, lamenting to my wife about money. She would ask me in exasperation if I ever thought or talked about anything other than bills and finances. I was like a man in mourning, grieving my loss, unable to see all the blessings surrounding me.

I defended myself by saying that I was preoccupied with money for the family's sake. But clearly, I was not actually focused on her or my children. I was always preoccupied with juggling those financial balls. After all, if I dropped even one, the rest would also be dropped with it.

I would always come up with some big plan to keep the balls in the air. They were about ideas — fantasies really — where I would recover and make millions. I am not a gambler, but as I look back, I realize I had a gambler mentality, acting like if I could just catch a lucky break, I would one day fully recover everything I had lost.

At those moments when I crashed, I would pray, begging God to help me out of the mess I had created. And He always did. But, once I was on my feet again, I would soon forget the help God had given me by coming to my rescue. Rather than learning to ask for God's help every day about every decision, I resumed my own course trusting myself as I again charged forward. I would even ask my wife if she thought I was making the right decision. She would give me an honest answer, saying "no". But I would go ahead and do it anyway. What disrespect! What idiocy! No wonder she got fed up with me!

All my Sunday School education didn't fully sink in. I never learned how to trust in the Lord with my whole heart and not lean on my own understanding. I didn't know how to acknowledge God in all my ways and let Him direct my paths. The whole warning to not be wise in my own eyes, to fear the LORD and depart from evil just didn't make sense to me. But if I had listened, I might have understood that fear of the Lord "will be health to your flesh, and strength to your bones" (see Proverbs 3:5–8).

This lesson I learned only through the school of hard knocks. How much easier and better would my life have been if I had turned to the Lord, not only when I was in trouble, but before I got myself in trouble! I just didn't seem to get it.

I did have the wealth of being loved by family and friends. They loved me no matter if I had material wealth or not. I could not understand that they would love me either way. I took that love for granted and thought that when I achieved material wealth, I would be secure in both love and money.

Chapter 7: Across the Miles

Taking a job in Australia added to our marriage problems as it was my decision to take the job in Australia.

I thought it would be a fabulous job which would get us back on our feet financially. When I went to check it out, the job was great. The country was amazing. I wanted my family to enjoy The Land Down Under with me. I wasn't seeking to live a bachelor life while my wife played single parent to our kids back in the States.

Reluctance

My wife was reluctant to relocate, however. We would be moving a long, long way from home. She was concerned that we might never come back or that the kids might very well fall in love with some Aussies, settle down, and never return to the USA.

She didn't want to uproot the family and leave everything she knew for the unknown. I admit that I had some concerns about moving to a country some 15,000 miles away, but I saw it as a great adventure. I would describe to her all the benefits in detail and offer arguments for how worthwhile it would all be. But in the end, she didn't want to buy it. She didn't want to move to Australia.

Although I didn't consider it at the time, I believe my wife may have felt as if I had been faced with a choice: my family in America or my job in Australia. It was like choosing one at the expense of the other. After some time of thinking and debating, I decided that I would go to Australia. It was a position at the pinnacle of my marketing career. I was grateful and excited about the opportunity and felt I had to take it.

The company I worked for in Melbourne was very generous. I purchased a 3500-square-foot penthouse which would have been plenty enough room for my wife and three kids to share with me. The company granted us five business-class round-trip tickets and four weeks of vacation per year. From my point of view, it was a once in a lifetime opportunity. Nevertheless, I did face a lot of guilt about moving away from my family. I might not have recognized it at the time, but it became a life-changing decision.

The Final Decision

The country's customs and patriotism brought back all my fondest childhood memories. They had terrific holiday parades and neighborhood barbeques. Being there was like going back in time. The culture reminded me of mid-twentieth-century Americana. It would have been a great place for us to spend time together as a family. It would have been an adventure. A wonderful place for the kids to grow and experience a whole new place.

I understand now that God had a plan allowing the situation to unfold the way it-did with me being away from my family. At the time, however, I struggled with the physical separation.

Perhaps I didn't understand that a relationship with family took more than checking in on special occasions and waiting to make memories together.

All I could see was that this was the biggest opportunity of a lifetime.

I went to Australia.

Part III

Do you ever think to yourself, "If I could do it all over again, I would do it all differently!"?

Do you reflect on the expanse of years behind you and wonder, "I've been a lot of places and done a lot of things, but what do I truly have to show for myself!"?

Do you think about how all you've done in this life is supposed to prepare you for the afterlife and worry, "How will my family and friends remember me? Have I really done all I can to show how much I love them? Have I done enough?"

I sure did once God showed me my life....

Chapter 1: Phantoms

The real trouble started when I sat down to dinner with my family after they came home from work. My wife and I were living in our son's house after we had declared bankruptcy.

I cautiously scooted my chair toward the dinner table since I had been experiencing severe back pain for the past couple of days. Suddenly, I noticed my brother and my mother sitting with me and my wife and son at the table.

I was happily chatting with these two when my son interrupted me to ask who I was talking to. Surprised at his question, I pointed out that Grandma and Uncle Dan were with us at the table. Now he was the one who looked surprised. He slowly explained that both had been deceased for years.

The Purple Haze

As I was contradicting him, insisting that the two other guests were right there at the table, my thoughts shifted away from my mother and brother. I now started seeing all kinds of colors swirling all around me: red, purple, and green. Not bright but hazy, like some sort of psychedelic experience. I mumbled to my family what was happening. They decided to take me to the hospital emergency room.

On the ride to the hospital, I noticed a man sitting in the left rear seat of the car. We engaged in a lengthy discussion. I didn't know the man but found him to be a great conversationalist. He seemed to know a lot about me. Was he perhaps my guardian angel? No one knew whom I was talking to. Whoever he was, I was the only one seeing and hearing him! I wish I could remember that conversation.

I don't remember anything after that.

I was taken to the emergency room and checked into the hospital. My family claims I was argumentative and obnoxious. It's likely that I was. As Reagan famously said, "I do not recall."

As a matter of fact, I had no recollection of the conversation with my mother and brother, the purple haze, the car ride, or the pain. I was not even aware that I was in the hospital.

I ended up in a coma.

Final Blow

How had I come across this hazy hallucination? No one could really explain what had led me up to this point. I had my suspicions though.

A few months earlier, I was residing in Australia, working for a global consulting firm, when I got an assignment to travel to Brazil. I had the background and experience to help with part of the project. It would take from four to six weeks to complete. The company put a team together, including me, and I began preparing for the assignment, both from a business perspective and a health perspective.

The assignment required traveling all over Brazil to enact due diligence on a chain of Brazilian businesses that a US company wanted to acquire. Having never been to Brazil, I thought I should get some vaccinations prior to leaving. I got every possible vaccination that I could, securing the health side of the assignment. Again, I sought security.

The assignment was completed in about six weeks. It was grueling because we had to travel all over Brazil. The long workdays took a toll on me. Plus, it didn't help that I was frequently going from a hot, humid climate outdoors to a freezing climate indoors. We had to go into cold, almost freezing rooms because that is how various cattle vaccines had to be stored. Consequently, our bodies frequently went from sauna heat to frigid cold when walking from the outdoors into the inventory medicine storage. To be sweating and then walk into an icebox may seem like fun, but the vast swing in temperature is not. Fortunately, I did not get sick from the experience.

The Brazilian assignment was completed, and I returned to Australia. I was there for a couple of weeks before returning to Michigan.

The Ax

One needs to have a strong work ethic to pursue wealth. I certainly had that. Within a week of coming back from Australia, I was living at my son's house and decided to do some work in his yard. Growing up on a farm in rural Wisconsin, I had always enjoyed being outside.

And I was pretty good at swinging an ax and chopping wood. A few years earlier, I had chopped down dozens of small trees around the yard to open it up and plant grass. First, the trees were cut down with a chain saw just at ground level. You want to avoid getting the chain on the saw in the dirt, as that immediately dulls the chainsaw.

Once the trees are cut, the ground is left with ground-level tree "stumps" that can hit the lawnmower blades when cutting. So, the stumps had been left there to start rotting before attempting to cut the grass around them. Since they had been left that way for a few years, I decided it was time to chop them up so the lawn could now be properly mowed.

I went into the garage and found a sharp ax that I could use to chop up the stumps. I didn't think it would be a difficult job. I also didn't think about the fact that I was in my late sixties and hadn't swung an ax in decades. But no worries, I could handle it. Or so I thought.

It never occurred to me that swinging the ax like a twenty-five-year-old lumberjack was probably not the best idea. I was not physically fit to even be attempting this project. Nevertheless, I continued chopping all day, determined to complete the job by nightfall. I completed the job alright. Miraculously, I did not chop right through my leg or foot.

Exhausted, I went to bed right after dinner and didn't wake up even once.

Back Ache

The next morning, I felt rested and refreshed. But my back hurt, and I had difficulty easing out of bed. Still, I got up and went downstairs to have breakfast. My back still hurt, and I assumed that I had strained or pulled some muscles which would probably feel better in a day or two. I had never had any back problems before so I figured there could be no other reason. I took a couple of Ibuprofens and went on about the day, feeling good that I'd finished the stump chopping job.

I started the riding lawnmower and began cutting the grass. The lawn expanded over quite a large area, so it took me over an hour to complete. I was feeling very proud that I could mow the entire lawn without any concern about the mower blades mower hitting a protruding low-level stump.

Upon finishing, I admired the freshly mowed lawn. I moved on to other projects, but the back pain continued. By the end of the day, it had become worse. I took more Ibuprofen. The pain dulled but continued.

I climbed into bed, hoping I'd feel better in the morning. I didn't.

When I woke up the next morning, the pain had become worse. As I tried to sit up and get out of bed, I could hardly move. I called my doctor and told him what was going on. He asked me to come into his office so he could examine me. I eased onto the examination table, lying flat on my back so he could check out what the issue might be. The doctor asked me to lift my left leg. I did that without any trouble. He then told me to lift my right leg. As I tugged the muscle controlling my right leg, I got an instant stabbing pain shooting through my back.

He did more examinations, advising me that I likely had strained my back muscles while chopping the stumps. He prescribed me some pain pills and sent me on my way.

By the third morning, my back pain was even worse. I couldn't even try to sit up in bed. I started thinking about how to help myself out of this near paralysis.

I gently rolled over and turned onto my stomach with my legs extended off the bed. I then began sliding myself off the bed and onto the floor. I pulled myself up to a sitting position, bracing myself with a chair.

Finally, sitting upright on the floor, I began using my arms to scooch myself toward the stairs that went to the main level of the house. The stairs were carpeted, so I began sliding down the stairs one at a time, just like a little kid, until I got down to the main level. I then used my arms again to help me scooch into the kitchen, where I finally pulled myself up onto a chair.

I took more pain pills, and slowly the pain subsided. I grabbed the remote and spent the next few hours painfully watching TV, trying to distract myself from the stabbing sensation in my back. Nothing really helped though. Within a couple of hours, the pain intensified.

Chapter 2: Toxicity

After my family had me checked into the hospital, they sat down with the medical team to explain what I had done. The wood chopping, the back pain, the walking difficulty, and the hallucinations. The doctors began examining me and running tests.

They found that I had sepsis in my bloodstream. It was traveling through my system and had settled in my spine, causing severe damage. The medical staff informed my family that I would need spinal surgery. Simultaneously, the staff would need to work on eliminating the sepsis infection.

My family learned that sepsis is an infection in the bloodstream and a serious medical condition. As a result, the infection travels throughout your entire body via your blood vessels. This dire surgery would be critical.

Sepsis results from an overwhelming immune response to infection. The body releases immune chemicals into the blood to combat the infection. Those chemicals then trigger widespread inflammation. If unchecked, the immune mediators trigger widespread inflammation, blood clots, and leaky blood vessels.

Such a situation ultimately impairs blood flow which thus damages organs by depriving them of nutrients and oxygen. In severe cases, organs begin to fail. In the worst cases, blood pressure drops, the heart weakens, and the patient spirals toward septic shock.

Spinal sepsis (also called spinal epidural or subdural abscess) is a rare condition which can lead to paralysis or death if not diagnosed rapidly. It is difficult to diagnose in its early stages as the symptoms are still non-specific.

Sepsis occurs unpredictably and can progress rapidly. Once this happens, multiple organs — lungs, kidneys, liver — may quickly fail in the person, causing death.

All the Little Things

Most sepsis is caused by bacterial infections. It can also be caused by viral infections, such as influenza, fungal infections, or noninfectious insults, such as traumatic injury. Normally, the body releases chemical or protein-immune mediators into the blood to combat the infection or insult.

Many types of microbes — various tiny little things — can cause sepsis, including bacteria, fungi, and viruses. However, bacteria are the most common cause. Severe cases of sepsis often result from a body-wide infection that spreads through the bloodstream.

In some cases, the bloodstream infection cannot be detected. In those cases, doctors use other information such as body temperature and mental status to diagnose sepsis. Sepsis often results from infections in the lungs, stomach, kidneys, or bladder. Sepsis can begin with a small cut that gets infected or an infection that develops after surgery. Sometimes, sepsis can occur in people who didn't know that they had an infection.

Last Chance

I share this medical information with you for one reason. It's not to show off all I have learned about an infection that plagued me and nearly caused me to die. I share it because it is a prime example of how vulnerable we are. How we could have our days numbered and not even be aware of our condition until it's too late.

We could be traveling to work one morning as we always do when we suddenly get into fatal a car accident. We could have a microscopic germ eating us alive from the inside. We could have an infection that our body overreacts to, and suddenly, we go unconscious while our family members are informed that we may have only a few hours left to live.

None of us is guaranteed tomorrow. That's why today is such a precious gift.

Anyone can get an infection, and almost any infection can lead to sepsis. Some people are at higher risk of infection and sepsis, like adults who are 65 or older. People with chronic medical conditions such as diabetes, lung disease, cancer, and kidney disease carry a higher risk too. Anyone with a weakened immune system is more prone than others to sepsis. That includes children under 12 months old.

I had never heard of sepsis. Nor did I understand the severity of my infection until after I was out of the hospital. As a diabetic over age 65, I fit the criteria for being a prime candidate susceptible to a sepsis infection.

My blood sugar issues, and advanced age were not the only factors leading me down this path.

My worldwide travel also put me in places where I would forego treatment if I got a small cut or scrape. A month prior to my infection, I had been traveling in remote areas of Brazil and was exposed to insect bites and a few minor cuts from the work I was doing. The infection might have also found a way into my body through my finger pricks for blood sugar checks. Or through the insulin injection site.

Although the doctors deemed it unlikely that Brazil and bug bites or finger pricks and injections triggered the sepsis, the medical staff were never able to identify the specific cause of my infection.

A person usually does not even know that they have sepsis since, typically, there is no pain. It insidiously travels through the person's bloodstream, infecting everything in its path. Slowly, it infects major organs and parts of the body. By the time the infection is discovered, it is often too late for any type of treatment. The person faces a critical diagnosis and must prepare for death.

I had never thought about death much before that hospitalization. You would think I would have considered it more with all the time I spent thousands of feet off the ground. Sure, I had life insurance to ensure that my family was taken care of should anything happen to me. But I had not really thought about death. I had spent little time reflecting on my life and thinking about the rap sheet I had created. I didn't dwell much on how I would face my maker and answer for myself once I got to the Pearly Gates.

Little did I know that my time was in danger of swiftly ending. I was hardly aware that the dinner I had enjoyed with my wife and son and my phantom mother and brother might well have been my last. By the time I got to the hospital, the infection had indeed traveled through my entire bloodstream seeking a place to settle and cause damage.

Life Saver

The infection found a nice little spot to camp in my spine. That's why I had the severe back pains. The back pains were not the result of chopping the tree stumps with the ax. On the contrary, the ax is probably what saved my life. In many cases, a person that has sepsis does not feel any pain because the infection is traveling through the bloodstream, slowly inflicting damage. Then, one day you can just collapse from the damage that has been done. That's what happened in my case. I had no symptoms.

I thank God that I was chopping wood and found my back hurting. I am grateful that I began hallucinating, which scared my family enough to take me to the emergency room.

By the time doctors discovered the sepsis in my spine, it had already done enough damage to require immediate surgery to repair and strengthen the infected vertebrae.

The hope was that the surgical team could first get all the infection out of that area. The subsequent surgical process was to build a permanent "cage" around my spine using six metal rods. This cage would strengthen my spine and help me lead a normal life doing most activities that I enjoyed doing.

The main concern was that the doctors might not be able to remove the infection completely. If they were unable to get it all, a second surgery would be required, which would be even more difficult and dangerous. They would not know until sometime later while I recovered over the next month.

A neurosurgeon led the surgery with his team. This was the best route to take since research showed that if the surgery was performed by a neurosurgeon and an orthopedic surgeon working together, patients were three times less likely to develop major complications such as wound infections, deep vein thrombosis, pulmonary embolism, and urinary tract infections.

The hospital called my family on several occasions because they were unsure that I would make it through the night. Members of my family stayed in my room with me for several nights, watching and praying for my recovery.

Meanwhile, an infectious disease specialist and her team were summoned to examine the infection still traveling through my bloodstream and attempt to get it under control. This involved utilizing various antibiotics injected into my bloodstream and monitoring their effectiveness. Since every person's immune system is different, they had to determine the best antibiotic treatment for me. This process had to be monitored over several weeks to ensure that they determined the right medication that worked for me.

I was hooked to a ventilator and in a coma while all this was happening. I had undergone serious spine surgery, and I still had sepsis running through my bloodstream. The doctors had told my family that the medical team had concerns about whether they had the sepsis under control with antibiotics. If they couldn't get the sepsis under control, it would continue to travel through my bloodstream, compromising my organs and my entire body.

I would likely die.

If they did get the sepsis under control, the doctors were still concerned about potential damage to several organs and body functions. Their concerns included determining if my kidneys, my liver, and other vital organs would continue functioning normally. And, of course, would there be any brain damage?

They further advised my family that they did not want to be forced to go back and have another operation. Chances were not good that I would live through that. Furthermore, if the antibiotics did not stop the sepsis from spreading through my system again, there was not much else that they could do.

The doctors would need to watch and wait. I spent three weeks in intensive care. The medical team continued monitoring me and studying if things were moving in a good direction.

Getting a sepsis infection under control is not an easy task. My team consisted of critical-care physicians and infectious disease physicians. nephrologists, neuroradiologists, urologists, and intensivists also looked after me.

Amazingly, I survived the intensive care experience. I have no recollection of that whole time frame, so I have had to reconstruct it after the fact. Following intensive care, I was moved to a rehabilitation center, where I would spend the next three months.

By the time they transferred me by ambulance, I was conscious and able to communicate somewhat. This began a whole new recovery process which included physical therapy, occupational therapy, speech therapy, and psychological therapy.

Essentially, it was almost like starting my life over. Having spent the better part of a month in a coma and intensive care, both my physical and mental health had deteriorated.

Chapter 3: Journey to the Unknown

Clearly, being in a coma for eight days, I had no knowledge of what was going on. No recollection of going into the hospital, no knowledge of the surgery, and no awareness of what day or time it was. Virtually, I had no understanding of anything going on outside of me.

In a way, it was like being in a cocoon. I was shielded from the outside world. Yet I was experiencing amazing transformations within.

But something was going on inside of me. Not physically but mentally. At some time during the comatic state, I began "dreaming." At first, it was a hazy process. It was like the opening scene of a movie where the camera initially struggles to gain focus. Viewing these dreams sort of felt like watching a movie. I could see every scene, but no one could see me.

Performance

The first scene appeared to be the outside of a theatrical playhouse. Not a movie theater, but a wooden structure made of beautiful, dark-stained wood. I could see the door, but not the inside.

People were milling around, getting ready for the play. There seemed to be a great deal of concern if everything was ready for the play.

There was some discussion about needing cushions to sit on. My wife volunteered to go and get the cushions from her store. Evidently, she owned a store selling cushions. She picked up and studied multiple cushions trying to make up her mind.

She then decided to make the needed cushions herself in various sizes and colors. She made some of the cushions using patterned cloth in various designs. One design was floral, but not with bright, colorful flowers. The flowers were brownish against a tan background. Another cushion had geometric images. It also came in various shades of brown but with a beige background. Somehow, the cushions were taken to the theater. Some of the logic of the dream is not totally clear.

Above It All

The scene shifted to me suddenly finding myself in the downtown area of a large city. I saw tall buildings and other structures. Unlike a city, there was no noise. And there were no people.

All I could see were structures and a city skyline. My view was from a high position where I was looking down at the buildings. It was as if I was looking out of a hotel window from a very high floor and observing the city. Yet, I was not standing on a floor or firm ground. I was just sort of floating, suspended above it all. Again, it was like I was an observer. The scenes were all playing in my mind but very, very real.

Going Down

The scene suddenly switched again. Now I was in what appeared to be some sort of large concrete structure. It was somewhat like a multi-story concrete parking structure but with high ceilings. I observed myself standing there, looking around.

I realized that it was not a parking garage. I was standing in an enormous room with concrete outside walls. There were no windows. It was quite a large building.

Then I noticed a big machine in the center of the room. It looked like a drab green oil derrick, with a large arm extending up from its top. A huge piston connected to the arm that was pumping up and down. The piston portion would go into a large cylindrical hole in the ground.

It reminded me of the piston in a car engine, except much, much larger, perhaps fifteen feet high and five feet in diameter. Just like the arm on an oil derrick, it just kept lifting and down. The same motion and rhythm, over and over.

However, the difference between an oil derrick and this machine is that this had a big piston head connected to it. The piston would go down into the large cylindrical hole. The cylinder was lined with metal so that the piston would fit snuggly against it as it rose and plunged into the hole.

The hole appeared to be four to five feet in diameter – large enough for a person to fit inside. The piston was designed to push down into the cylinder, then come up and out for about six feet. Then it would slowly plunge down into the cylinder and then come up again. The whole process just kept going on mechanically, over and over. It seemed like the pumping cycle would never end.

The machine made a muted squishing sound each time the piston plunged into the cylinder. The only sound was the squishing as it kept its constant up-and-down movement.

I also noticed a fog-like cloud – a green misty haze – that enveloped only the area of the pumping piston. It was difficult to see the piston clearly. For whatever reason, the cloud hung only around the machine. It didn't envelop the entire massive room I stood in.

I felt that perhaps I should look at the machine from a different angle.

A Different View

In the next scene, I was standing on a large concrete platform, positioned about twenty feet from the front of the piston so I could observe it plunging in and out of the cylinder. From that different angle, I saw the same slow rhythm, heard the same squishing sound, noticed the same eerie, greenish smog.

I also noticed something else. A line.

A long line of human bodies extended out from the concrete wall and into another room. They, too, were in a slight greenish-gray haze, but the color differed slightly from the smoggy haze around the pumping piston.

The human figures did not look like real-life humans. Rather, they were dull and muted. Their features were difficult to detect, almost like looking at silhouettes. Yet, they were three-dimensional. All of them were grown adults; no children were in that line.

The figures just kept advancing straight ahead. It was a slow, slight movement. No arms swinging or heads turning. Only legs shuffling, trudging one step in front of the other. They made no expressions. They uttered no sounds. They were practically zombie-like in appearance and mannerism. They seemed lifeless, although they were still alive. They were walking ever so slowly toward the piston.

I'm not sure if they knew their fate. They walked one right after the next in a single, endless line.

A morose mood filled the scene. The stark room was eerily quiet. Everything about the place felt gloomy, dirty, and dim. The place was not totally dark. However, it contained a darkness that made the scene even more miserable.

I didn't want to join that line. I didn't want to stay at all.

I surmised that I wanted to be anywhere else. At that instant, I noticed something that I had not seen before: a mysterious green smog around the plunger tip and the hole opening.

Then I noticed where the line was heading. As the plunger retracted to its peak height, the next human stepped up and fell into the pit. They were not being pushed. They just toppled into the pit. The piston-plunger plummeted after them – *squish* – crushing the body as it lurched downward.

Sometimes, the people advancing would fall partially into the hole. The piston would plunge downward. Any dangling limbs would be dragged along.

The was no screaming. No blood-curdling howls of terror. No protests, defenses, or pleading excuses. No wailing and gnashing of teeth even.

Only humming. The humming of the machine as it went up and down. And squishing. The squishing of each body being crushed at the bottom of the pit.

Over and over, the piston-plunger pulled back out of the cylinder shaft. Over and over, it lurched downward. Another human stepped forward into the pit. Another squish sounded as the body got crushed at the bottom.

Plunge, *squish*.

Plunge, *squish*.

Plunge, *squish*.

Plunge, *squish*.

Plunge, *squish*.

The cycle kept going and going endlessly. I somehow understood that.

I stood there, panicked. I couldn't move. I couldn't speak. I needed to escape. I had to get out of there fast. As fast as I could! I ran.

I ran away from the machine. Away from the plunging. Away from the endless human line. Away from the squishing sound. Away from everything I had witnessed.

I ran as far as I could go. I ran in a large circle, avoiding the machine but sensing that I was being drawn toward it, drawn into it.

I kept running and running. The machine kept plunging and plunging. There had to be a way out of this fate. I did not want to die.

Please, Lord, don't let me die!

Chapter 4: Why Are We Here?

My running ceased. I had entered a new scene. The mood was subdued and somber. I noticed a partially opened doorway through which I could see some people quietly speaking with each other. The mood seemed very solemn.

I saw my family members engaged in a quiet conversation. Some of them were talking with other people in the room. Others were talking to each other with sad looks on their faces. Some of them walked up to the casket and stood there. Some cried.

Flower bouquets lined the outside walls. Larger clusters of flowers were placed on cascading stands at each side of the casket. The softly lit room entreated a sense of respect and peace.

I wondered what had brought together all these people, many of whom I was familiar with. Then I noticed something that I did not expect to see. It was me.

I was lying in a coffin at the front of the room. Everyone had gathered for a funeral. Mine.

Interesting, the person I saw in the casket was a younger version of myself, with a full head of hair, neatly combed. I wore a double-breasted, lightly pinstriped blue suit with a red tie. It reminded me of the many meetings I had attended for over forty years in my various business roles. Here, I was dressed for a meeting of another kind. An afterlife meeting!

At least I looked sharp, I thought. Wouldn't want to meet St. Peter looking out of place!

I noticed someone holding a Bible. Not my Bible, but my grandfather's Bible. I had never seen my grandfather's Bible, so I was confused why that Bible, not my own, was there.

The other thing I noticed was my funeral bulletin. As someone was reading it, I saw my name inside along with my date of birth but not my date of death.

Why would there be a funeral unless I was dead?

Chapter 5: Silence

I was in a completely new place: the most beautiful field of flowers I had ever seen.

All around me were flowers of every color, swaying gently in the wind. The colors were incredibly vivid. It was like a beautiful rainbow of colors. There was no specific species of flower I noticed, just a vast field of indescribable beauty.

Peaceful and quiet and absorbing. An exquisite cloudless blue sky was showing overhead. I walked through the endless flowers, relaxed, happy, and content.

As I slowly walked along, I started thinking about where I might be. I had some awareness that I might be dead. I still appeared to be conscious but in a different sort of way. I must be dead. They had a funeral for me. I had never heard of a place like this. Maybe God gives you some time after you die to walk around and enjoy the world's true beauty. To "stop and smell the flowers," so to speak.

Memories of life began to well up in my conscious. The first time I experienced an event involving such finality was my high school graduation.

Graduation

After my graduation ceremony, I celebrated like all the other grads. What was a proper celebration without alcohol? That afternoon and long into the evening, I consumed more than my share.

The next morning, I felt lousy, suffering my first hangover. My father took no pity on me. Instead, he played "Reveille" on his Army bugle as loud as he possibly could. With a pounding head and a nauseous stomach, I stumbled into the kitchen where he was waiting for me.

I anticipated a lecture on the evils of drinking, followed by some tough farm work just to make the hangover sink into my alcohol-induced sickness. I was certain my father wanted to teach me a lesson.

"Rough night?" he asked me. I didn't answer. He waited. I waited. No lecture came. Just the observation, followed by a question.

"So now that you've graduated, what are you going to do to take care of yourself?" He stared at me. I blinked at him, silent. I had no answer.

My head hurt. It was hard to think straight. What was I going to do now? I hadn't thought of it much. I had only thought about writing my final papers, taking my last class exams, getting to the graduation ceremony, drinking with my friends. I hadn't thought about what I was going to do after the party was over. After my head stopped hurting.

His piercing gaze subsided, allowing the question to hang in the air. Those were the only words he spoke to me.

I stood embarrassed, knowing that I could not answer my father for my future.

This question was his polite way of telling me that I had earned the honor of being on my own financially. Therefore, I should no longer rely on him to foot my bills.

By today's standards, that might seem harsh. Yet, I didn't feel like he was kicking me out. My father was a good man – faith and education were his top priorities. He supported my ideas and wanted me to succeed. Practically speaking, my father had his own financial challenges and needed me to take responsibility for myself. However, he also felt it was good and proper for a young man to make his own way in life. He was cutting the tether to home and allowing me to forge my own way.

Life Reflection

In the endless field of flowers, I reflected on my life. I thought of how I had forged my way. All the things I had done to support myself. The ways I had taken responsibility for myself. Or shirked the responsibility that should have been mine to handle.

While I considered all these aspects of my life, I noticed the multitude of colors surrounding me. When considering my life, the only color that stood out was green: money. I had been determined to get as much of it as I could. The pursuit of wealth had been my life's work.

What a waste. Money had absolutely no value in this place of peace and beauty. Not green, gold, or silver.

A verse from Ecclesiastes notes that each man enters and leaves the world with nothing: "This also is a grievous evil, that in all points as he came, so shall he go. And what profit does he have who labors for the wind?" (Ecclesiastes 5:16). I felt the emptiness of my hands in this moment. The nakedness of my soul. My spirit grew profoundly humbled.

As I continued to walk along, enjoying the beautiful flowers, I noticed a building on a small hill off in the distance to my left. As I got closer, I could see that the building was white.

It was an oblong building with the long side facing me. The sloped roof pitched a little more than a house roof and seemed to have cedar shingles. There was no steeple, so it did not appear to be a church.

I saw no windows, yet a bright light streamed out the front of the building. The light beaming forth was indescribably brilliant.

I continued to walk toward the building on the hilltop. I was literally "drawn to the light," which was becoming more and more brilliant. Intense and vibrant, I had never seen anything like it. It was not like sunlight. It was pure light. That's the only word to describe it.

The light was drawing me forward. I wanted to get closer to it. I wanted to be part of that brilliance, that magnificence. The light was too bright and majestic for me to feel as if I truly belonged there. But I wanted to be nearer to it, to have it encompass me.

As I continued to be drawn to the light, I found myself standing on top of the hill. The light shone from the building doorway to my left. The dazzling rays seemed to shine right through my body.

I just stood there, letting the light permeate through me. I was frozen in place. But this time, my paralysis was not from fear. I was in awe. I was staring straight ahead but was so astounded that I did not even see what was out in front of me. My mind was fixated on that light beaming right through me.

I experienced something like a catatonic state, where I could see inside myself. I could visualize the inside of my mind. My physical body was there, but I felt somehow transparent. I could look inside myself and "see" my mind and thoughts clearly. Words were "forming" inside my head. I thought about speaking, but I couldn't form the words. I was just there. I could catch the brilliant light shining through me to my right out of the corner of my eye.

I attempted to look toward the door to my left. I barely saw a doorway because the light's intensity obscured everything around it.

I instinctively knew that God was inside the room. I turned away.

I tried to imagine what He might look like, but I was terrified to even think of it. My mind a blank. I just stood there. The rays beamed through my whole body at a 45-degree angle straight down to the earth. Several minutes seemed to pass, but I'm not sure how long it really was.

My head snapped back to where I was looking forward again. But my forward vision was inside my head and consciousness, not whatever the scenery was directly in front of me. The whole occurrence was like an out-of-body experience where I was observing myself.

Standing in the light, I knew that God Himself was gazing upon me. Perhaps He was just inside that doorway. Perhaps He was the light. I can't accurately describe it. I had a certainty, though, that I was in His presence.

I sensed that God would be asking me about my life. I felt like He held the Book of Life right there and was turning the pages to my name.

Facing His brilliance and majesty, the first thoughts that came to mind were the sins I had committed in my life. These failings appeared in my stream of thought. They flowed out of me, and I could not hide them. They were all there in front of me. Every single one of them. It was a long list, some sins more significant than others.

As I pondered them, I briefly thought that perhaps I could hide them or even lie about them! One thing I knew for certain was that God detests liars. So, I immediately nixed that idea.

Just then, I heard a loud booming voice.

Tom, what have you done with the talents that I gave you to do My work?

I did not have an answer.

Those are the only words He spoke to me. The piercing light vanished, allowing the question to hang in the air. I blinked, silent. I had no answer.

I stood ashamed, knowing that I could not answer God for my life.

Tears began streaming down my face as I viewed my sins and wished I could erase them all. I knew that I couldn't. Could I somehow go back to the world and replace the bad with some good?

In retrospect, I wonder if God left me there alone so I could really dig deep inside myself and contemplate my life.

Every time I recount the story of God asking me what I had done for Him with the gifts that He gave me, I tear up and start sobbing. My whole self-fills with emotion, and I struggle to say anything. I recall the intense shame of that moment. I knew deep inside that I had not answered God's call to me.

At the time, it felt like I had been faced with a choice: living a serious, practical life with limited fun in my limited little town or living the good life filled with novel experiences while exploring the world.

I might have seen that I could have somehow fulfilled God's call to some form of ministry while also traveling and encountering new cultures. Maybe God had been calling me to more of a missionary field. Perhaps he didn't want me in a pastor's role at all.

Perhaps if I had fostered a heart to help others, I could have used my wealth to benefit others instead of just collecting more luxuries and toys. God did always seem to answer my prayer for a good-paying job. Maybe he was just giving me chance after chance to do something with it that would serve His Kingdom and not just myself.

I might have followed a path that would have allowed me to be with my family more. Develop deeper relationships with others. Be more fulfilled as a person. If I had worked on being the person God had wanted me to be, I might have grown into a stronger family leader. I might have left a stronger legacy to my children.

Perhaps I didn't understand that a relationship with God took more than asking when times get tough and receiving His blessing so I could get my life back to normal.

All I could see was that I needed to take charge of my life and sometimes God's help came in handy.

I just continued my own path.

Chapter 6: Silver and Gold

My journey was not yet over. The scene changed again. I could now see straight out in front of me. I became aware that I was standing on a hilltop, looking down into a valley of treetops. The view was extraordinarily clear and green. The colors were more vivid than any in real life.

Stretching out before me, I saw a beautiful green panorama that cascaded down the hill where I was standing and off into the distance toward another hill.

The Silver Road

As I stood there, I noticed a road to my right, curving back into the distance. I recognized that the road was a solid silver road, shining and glistening brilliantly. The road started to come into clear focus. It was like some sort of unveiling process began. I started seeing things positioned on the road in front of and going off into the distance.

I began to recognize the objects. They were also solid silver like the road. They looked somewhat like monopoly pieces but in intricate, detailed form — precisely as they had appeared to me in real life.

I saw the Corvette I had loved. I had idolized Corvettes from the time I was a kid. I had begged my father to let me buy one and co-sign on the loan and insurance. Being a sixteen-year-old kid, I'm sure my father thought I was out of my mind. He just said, NO!

"When you make your own money, you can buy a Corvette yourself," he told me. I did just that. I'm sad to say that the Corvette has been an idol of mine for my entire adult life. I became so paranoid about losing it that I quit driving it and kept it covered in the garage! Early in life, I drove the car every day in any kind of weather. Later, however, my fear hindered my sense of adventure. I was so concerned about damaging the vehicle that I drove it out of the garage only to wash and wax it. It became my beautifully immaculate, hidden treasure that no one saw or appreciated except me.

As I stood there, I also noticed the other things I had lusted after and bought: Cadillacs, Mercedes, Porsches, SUVs, houses, a ski boat, a cabin cruiser, snowmobiles, jet skis, and other material items. All were displayed in solid silver, just like Monopoly pieces. They were just things, inanimate, and not of much value.

Witnessing my collection of hoarded treasures on this road, I began wondering why I had ever esteemed them so much. Why had I felt like I had to have them? Why had I devoted my hard-earned money and my precious time to purchasing them, caring for them, protecting them?

I thought of Jesus' admonishment, warning people to guard themselves from greed, since life's value doesn't depend on the material items which we have stored for ourselves. The Lord continued, telling the parable of the Rich Fool who sought to build bigger barns for his property and store surplus grain so he could live easy. God accused the man of foolishness, revealing that he would soon be required to give an account of his life, and all those things he had accumulated would quickly go to someone else. Ultimately, a person "who lays up treasure for himself" is "not rich toward God" (see Luke 12:15, 20-21).

I realized that this silver road represented materialism. I had been following it most of my life. However, when God asked about my life, telling Him that I had accumulated a bunch of material things was a laugh. God owns everything, everywhere.

I began to clearly see that focusing on material things may impress people at stoplights.

However, they certainly wouldn't impress the Sovereign Lord of Heaven and Earth.

The Gold Road

Next, I looked to my left. I saw a gold road, stretching out the same identical way as the silver one, curves and all. Immediately I noticed what was different between the two roads besides the gold and silver color. On that road was something completely different: people.

People were on that road. They stood either alone, in pairs, or in groups. I could tell that some were even in love with each other, holding hands or wrapping their arm across the other person's shoulder. The ones in groups appeared to be communicating with each other. The figures seemed to be enjoying each other's company.

This road seemed to be paved with relationships, people connecting heart to heart, spirit to spirit.

As I watched, I wondered who these people might be and what they were talking about. Were they my family or friends? Were they people who were good to me whom I could have learned from if I had spent more time with them? Were they the homeless people at the traffic light holding a cardboard sign pleading for help while I drove away? Were they lonely people who needed my guidance but whom I ignored? I have pondered this question many times. Still, I don't know the answer.

Whoever they were, the people on the gold road seemed happy. I heard no noise or laughter, but they had an aura of happiness around them. I wondered if I had ever followed that road for a time in my life. And if I had, why did I ever leave?

After some hard thinking, I realized that I had been on the spiritual road during brief periods in life. Yet, the time I had spent there was not anywhere close to how frequently I had been on the materialism road. The number of "items" on the silver materialism road far outweighed the number of "people" on the gold road, which I will call the spiritualism road.

A horrific disappointment in my life choices enveloped me. I felt steeped in sadness. Imagine focusing more on materialism and objects rather than on the wonders of other humans! What had I been chasing after all these years! Had any of it brought me true joy or peace? I thought about how God created humans in His image while material things were created by man.

How could I have been so stupid! And now, here I stood in front of God, trying to explain what I had done with the gifts He had given me. I knew that I had no answer. No acceptable answer at all.

I stared ahead at the two roads stretching off into the distance. I stood there alone, considering my life.

I began praying that I could change my life going forward.

I awoke from my coma!

Chapter 7: New Dawn, New Day

The first thing I heard was people talking to me. I had no idea where I was, how I had gotten there, or what had happened. I knew only that I was alive. God had given me another chance!

But, while I was no longer in a coma, I was still in intensive care for several weeks. I was very weak and lost my weight and muscle strength. I was transferred to a rehabilitation hospital, where I spent the next three months. There was concern over my physical and cognitive abilities, so I underwent occupational, physical, and mental therapy. I was so weak, that I was unable to walk by myself.

The medical staff started by helping me to just sit up. That was suddenly a major challenge. We practiced for a short period every day, until I could do it on my own. Next, they brought a walker. I realized that I could not even stand up.

Just like a baby, at first, I needed help. I needed people to hold me up and keep me from falling. Then I could do a little bit with a walker. Then I could do a little bit on my own. Then I could do a little more.

Bit by bit, I began to figure it out. Little by little, I gained independence. I can't tell you how amazing it was to walk on my own for the first time.

I began walking in the hallway outside my room. It was a circular building. I discovered that walking twenty-five "loops" around the inside aisle of the circular rehab building was equal to one mile. Then, to walk a mile. Then five miles!

I don't recall how thrilled I was the first time I learned to walk as a one-year-old, but the excitement of relearning how to walk as a sixty-nine-year-old! It felt like being a kid all over again!

I also learned to pray.

I learned to thank God and to listen for His guidance. I thanked God for the gift of life. I thanked Him for every little milestone I crossed. I thanked him for every tiny success and that I had good people looking after me.

I began reading my Bible each day. I would read the passages and then pray about them. Over time, I found myself communicating with God differently. I reflected a lot on when I stood before Him and when He asked me what I had done with the gifts He had given me.

I gave a lot of consideration to how I could live my life differently during my remaining years.

Fortunately, part of my recovery therapy involved psychological help as well. I discussed my feelings with a psychologist and shared my experiences before and after entering the hospital. I worked on sorting through my feelings. I had fears of not being able to do things that I had always been able to do. I also had some depression and frequently became emotional. I often cried and wasn't sure how the rest of my life would be changed, if at all. The whole recovery process drained me physically, mentally, and emotionally.

Spiritual Awakening

When laying in the hospital bed and reviewing my life, it became clearer and clearer that I had not done much of anything spiritually. I reflected on how my focus had been geared toward materialistic pursuits. The realization was a very uncomfortable feeling, and I began thanking God for His mercy and all His blessings. I began asking Him for guidance going forward.

The entire experience of the dreams and the recovery had my head spinning. The process had given me a lot to consider about what I would do with the rest of my life.

Finally, after three months, the day came when I was released from the rehabilitation hospital and could go home.

I thanked all the dedicated medical experts who had given me my life back. They had become friends. One of the nurses gave me a beautiful neck scarf that she had made herself. I would miss those people who had become a daily part of my life when I was most vulnerable. Like any transition, leaving the hospital carried a mix of happy and sad sentiments.

My habit of praying and my commitment to exercising my body and mind had paid off. I left the rehab center on my own, walking out that front door to the car that would take me home. I had entered the hospital on September 17th. I went home in the late afternoon of December 23rd just in time to spend Christmas at home. I am eternally grateful.

Chapter 8: Immensely Grateful

Where do I go from here? How do I deliver on the gifts God gave me so that when we meet again, I will have an answer to His question?

At my age, I believe that the next meeting may well be the final meeting on Judgement Day. I've come to realize that life's journey is really a preparation for our eternal journey. I want to do everything I can do to prepare for that day and the eternity after judgment.

My experience has humbled me tremendously. I am deeply grateful for every blessing every day.

The thing that I am most grateful for is losing everything. God knew that I would not get the message any other way. I needed to lose it all to find Him.

I am reminded of Job's words about coming into the world and going out of it naked, with nothing. Indeed, the Lord gives and takes away. Yet, like Job, I shall choose to bless the name of the Lord (see Job 1:21).

It took me losing everything to find the one thing that was most important: my faith. I had focused on acquiring material things my whole life. Yet, when all those things were stripped away, I realized how truly blessed I was. When all the insignificant things had vanished, I was left with what was truly significant: God and my faith.

For once in my life, I quit trying to control everything. Some people might think I gave up, that I surrendered. I like to think of it this way: I handed over the steering wheel to someone who could steer me along a better path.

It was hard to let go. I was never a quitter. Giving up wasn't in me. I was not one to ever surrender. I had gripped that steering wheel for many decades of my life. Prying my fingers off of it took many acts of resolution.

I had to stop looking at how much I wanted to be in charge. Instead, I needed to start knowing God and trusting His desired path for me. Then the handoff became easier and easier. I became like a trusting child who happily takes his father's hand while walking down the road.

I found my mind clean, clear, and open to receive. God, in His infinite grace, was there with me. The instant I said, "God, I give up," I felt God's presence. He immediately answered my prayers and blessed me with a new job.

God's Providence was obvious and immediate. A job that I would never have thought of was suddenly available to me. It was a great job. I enjoyed the work, and it paid very well.

I made enough money to pay back every cent I couldn't pay when I had gone bankrupt. I was grateful to no longer be indebted to anyone. The freedom of financial independence made me astoundingly joyful.

Because I had declared bankruptcy, I was not legally required to pay everything back. But in my mind, it was the right thing to do. It brought me peace.

During the bankruptcy process, one of my friends asked me how I could maintain such a positive attitude. He said that I was always in good spirits even amid financial ruin. Well, I did have my moments of fear, anger, and regret. I just tried not to show them.

I felt that something else was going on inside me. Looking back on it, I was letting go of one thing and it was being replaced by another, even better, thing. A spiritual awakening.

I believe that bankruptcy was a turning point in my life where I realized that material things are not God's purpose for my life. He has forgiven me for my bad financial choices. He blesses me with more than I could have ever imagined.

Truly, God has helped me recover financially, but more importantly, He has led me to spiritual recovery. Healing my spirit — reclaiming my soul for the Lord — that is indeed the most important thing. He is giving me another chance at life. Praise the Lord!

What I'm getting back is a hundred-fold what I have lost. I've grown much closer to God. I've come to love God, and I work at keeping Him first in my life. I practice quieting myself and listening for His voice and direction.

I don't hear that booming voice I heard when He spoke to me during the coma. However, there is an inner voice that I listen for. I don't have the material things I once had, and I'm glad. I have something far better: a relationship with Father God and my Lord and Savior Jesus Christ.

I now stick post-it notes on my computers that read, "Help me, Jesus" because I don't ever want to forget that I need His help daily to steer me in the right direction.

I feel more blessed than I have ever felt in my life. When friends ask me how I'm doing, I always reply that I'm more blessed than stressed.

The Wonders of Life

I now start every morning excited to discover God's plan for me that day. It's like going on a new adventure each morning. I am truly grateful to start a new day. My morning ritual starts with reading my Bible. I had always wanted to read the entire Bible, and now I do it each year. My near-death experience took place in 2017. I'm in the fifth year of reading my Bible cover to cover.

I chose to use a 365-day Bible containing daily readings from the Old Testament, the New Testament, the Psalms, and the Proverbs. I'm amazed that new passages stand out to me every time I read God's Word. I highlight them and reflect on them. Perhaps, by the end of my life, I will have highlighted every passage in the Bible. Why not?

God has already spoken to me personally, so I want to absorb His Word. If I never read another book again, it won't matter; God's Word has every answer I need for my daily life. It is my daily bread.

Seven Things a Day

Aside from Bible reading, I also list seven things I am grateful for each day.

I chose seven for a few reasons.

Seven is a Biblical number. According to *The Meaning of Numbers*, the Number 7 is used 735 times (54 times in the book of Revelation alone). The number seven is the foundation of God's Word. If we include with this count how many times 'sevenfold' (6) and 'seventh' (119) are used, our total jumps to 860 references to the number seven.

Seven is also the number signifying completeness and perfection (physical and spiritual). Its meaning is tied directly to God's creation of all things. In my case, I've struggled with material versus spiritual pursuits, so I settled on seven as a very significant number in my life.

Furthermore, I believe seven is an achievable number of things to be grateful for each day. While we receive hundreds, perhaps thousands of blessings every day, I wanted to come up with a shortlist of the key things on my mind each day. Being grateful does not imply recounting every blessing you notice throughout the day. We are humanly unable to comprehend, remember, and document every single one of God's blessings. Often, we don't even recognize the blessings we're given: food, clothing, a clear sky, rain, air to breathe, glasses to help us see better, a band-aid, church, friends, a job, or a smile from a stranger. It's okay if we don't take note of all these things. God continues to bless us anyway.

The more you practice gratitude, the more you will notice all there is to be thankful for. At times, we will want to thank God especially for granting us the things we have been praying for. Other times, we'll want to offer thanks for the things that God, in His infinite wisdom, did not give us. Thank God for delivering us from ourselves!

Seven Is Easy to Do

Seven seemed like a practical and doable daily list. If you write down your seven items each day for 365 days, you will have thanked God for 2,555 things in a year. If we could do that for fifty years, we would thank God over 127,000 times! Imagine how God appreciates that.

God blesses us millions of times throughout our lives, so seven items a day becomes a minute sacrifice. Just as God is consistent in His blessings to us, we should be consistent in thanking Him every single day. It takes less than seven minutes to write down seven things you're thankful for. I believe God appreciates every thank you He receives.

Every Day Is Different

When I began writing down my seven things each day, I thought I would find myself just jotting down many of the same things daily. After doing this every day, every year, for some five years, I've learned that there are only a few items that I occasionally repeat. There are so many events in my life each day that I'm grateful for that I don't seem to have a problem with duplication. Every day is different, so those things I'm grateful for each day are also different.

I believe that communication with God needs to be done with our full concentration and attention. I'm convinced there's a connection between the mind and human hands and paper and pen or pencil. Somehow, my brain is wired that way. I'm a pretty good typist (I took typing as a subject in high school back in the day). Yet, if I really want to understand something and contemplate it, I find that a good old pencil and piece of paper are what work best for me.

I maintain a physical journal and write my grateful list in it every day. While I have never been a "journal person," I rarely miss a day of writing in my Grateful journal. I keep it a top priority for each day. When I do miss a day, I feel off-balance, like I didn't place God first that day.

I have completed a journal every year for the past five years and put them on my bookshelf. Periodically, I take the old journals out and read what I wrote on that day years before. I learn a lot about how my life has changed. I also learn how it has remained the same. I'm still grateful for many of the same things.

The Seven F's

To help me every day, I created an official list of seven categories that provide the foundation of my life:

- Faith
- Forgiveness
- Freedom
- Family
- Friends
- Finances
- Future

I put faith first because, without that, my life would be imbalanced. God's unconditional forgiveness allows me to start every day fresh and renewed. He forgives and forgets. He doesn't ruminate and maintain a list of every sin that I've committed. Praise God! How blessed are we to receive God's grace and mercy.

We are also blessed to have freedom. I've often taken my freedom for granted, but it is a real blessing. I have witnessed people who live in countries without political freedom; the human spirit does not thrive in such a society.

Even considering freedom on a more individual level, many things can take away our freedom; fear, greed, loss or addiction confines people from their ability to act freely. We should always seek freedom in mind, spirit, and society. We should also be ever so grateful for it.

Of course, family and friends are treasured gifts from God. Admittedly, I've sometimes also taken them for granted. I must remind myself how blessed I am to have them in my life. I cannot overstate their love and support in helping me through many of life's challenges.

Finances is a big category, which I am grateful for. It includes food, clothing, shelter, transportation, employment, and all the basics of living. I decided against the word "money" because money is only the tender for facilitating our basic needs.

I put future as the final category on my gratitude list because I'm excited about what blessings God has in store for me every day. The next 24 hours can be considered the future. We do not know what will happen for the rest of today, let alone this week, this month, or years down the road. Every minute of life in front of us is the future. Being grateful for the future sets our expectations for God's blessings in every upcoming moment.

Those are seven things combined into one line of my daily Grateful Journal that cover the basics of daily life. That is one line that I include in my journal each day. There is so, so much to be grateful for!

Chapter 9: Needing Only One Thing

I've become very committed to my routine of daily Bible reading, journaling seven grateful items, and offering my daily prayers. I like to think of that special time as my "Breakfast with God."

I get my morning coffee and settle into a comfortable chair to do my reading and writing. It's a quiet place where I can focus, concentrate, and listen. It's where I try to communicate with God. I want to hear what He wants me to do today. I'm not suggesting that God talks to me like He did in my near-death experience. Nevertheless, there is a spiritual closeness that quiet devotional time brings each morning.

I'm then excited to get my day going. I eagerly await what unfolds for me. I pray for the grace to follow God's path for me that day. I pray He will keep me on the path He has for me.

I've learned that communication with God is essential each day to bring me closer to Him. I'm trying to listen to Him instead of talking about what I need from Him. I need only one thing: closeness to God. He gives me all that He knows I need. Forget what I think I want. He gives us each day our daily bread. Not necessarily the sweets we desire.

I cannot imagine not being able to communicate with my Heavenly Father. He is with all of us 24 hours a day, 365 days a year. How grateful I am to have that direct access to God. Incredible!

That access is available to all the billions of people around the world. It's impossible to understand how God can communicate instantly and constantly with everyone around the world. You could say that the internet gives us a small taste of that capability today. Yet, we know that even the internet has its limitations. We cannot communicate with every person in the world simultaneously. Nor can we speak or understand every language. Even the most powerful man-made computer system cannot do that. Only God can.

He is also the only one who knows everything about each of us. We are assured that the Lord knew us before forming us in the womb and sanctified us before we were born (see Jeremiah 1:5).

How wonderful is that! Knowing that we were formed by the hands of a loving God who knew us before we came into existence is a singular concept that should make us grateful every minute of every day.

If you start your day by having "Breakfast with God" and writing down just seven things each day, you will ultimately recognize many things that you never noticed as blessings. The more grateful you become, the more you notice all the ways God blesses you.

The Bible also makes it clear that we should have a grateful heart. We are encouraged to give thanks in everything (see 1 Thessalonians 5:18).

One of the most recognized gratitude prayers is the prayer of Jabez in 1 Chronicles 4:10 where Jabez called upon the God of Israel, asking for His blessing. He asked specifically that the Lord would increase his boundaries, that God's hand would be with him, and that the Lord would keep him from evil so that he would not cause pain. Jabez's prayer pleased the Lord, for the passage assures us that "God granted him that which he requested."

I have prayed the prayer of Jabez in the past. I thought that it would help me get more money. More financial security. Maybe praying it would even help me win the lottery. Clearly, I was praying for myself, treating God as a billionaire who could easily spare a few million for me.

I don't pray for money anymore. The problem was that when God gave it to me, and although He did bless me with a lot of money, I spent it on the things that would build up my kingdom, not His.

Today, I tithe. For me personally, I have come to really enjoy giving. That's a new experience for me. At first, I was scared, wondering how I could afford tithing on top of all my other bills. However, I continue to follow the guidance given in 2 Corinthians 9:7 to give cheerfully, according to what I have determined in my heart. For His part, God continues to generously bless me for being generous to others.

I decided that everything in the world is His already. So, why would I not give back gratefully just ten percent of what He has blessed me with? Sometimes I think, no, *I can't afford it this week, so I'll skip it.* And I have skipped it occasionally when I feel hard-pressed. But I do try and make it up.

I no longer worry about money. While I don't have much, I always manage to get by. Every time I have had a "financial emergency," I have trusted in God, and He has provided. He has provided money from sources that I would never have imagined. Amazingly, the blessing of Providence is always just the right amount to cover the financial emergency. It's uncanny. I have learned to trust Him. I remain very grateful.

Since I began my daily prayers by thanking God for things instead of asking for things, my days have gone more smoothly than ever before. I am in a better mood. I am eager to start the day. I am excited to discover God's plan for me today.

I no longer waste time ruminating about the past. I remember my past, but I am not obsessed with the fears I had then. Nor am I preoccupied with how to retrieve the good times I had. Today the past does not rule my decisions in a reactionary way. I value it because I have learned from it. But it does not control me. Some lessons were very challenging. Hopefully, I will not need to learn them over again.

A grateful heart and soul have given me a new lease on life. I like to say that when I am grateful, I'm also joyful, which makes me peaceful.

You can't be grateful and ungrateful for the same thing at the same time. You can't be joyful and sorrowful over the same issue at the same time. Nor can you be peaceful while you are upset.

I keep it simple with these three words:

Grateful. Joyful. Peaceful.

Chapter 10: The Final Question

This is the story is of me as a young man hearing deep inside myself a calling to serve God developing relationships and following spiritualism. I ignored it. For sixty years, I spent most of my waking hours serving a different god: materialism.

It's a story of God giving me two near-death experiences, trying to get me back on the right road.

It's a story of me answering God's calling some sixty years after I heard it the first time at age 12.

It's a story about using the gifts that God gave me for His purpose, not mine. Using my God-given talents not for the sake of making my own kingdom more glorious but for bringing glory and honor to the Almighty while building up God's Kingdom.

And it's the story of learning the importance of gratefulness to live a life of joy and peace. To focus on what really matters in life. Not prestige. Not power. But people. And prayer. And precious moments are granted to me each day.

Not all of us are called to be ministers. Frankly, in retrospect, I don't believe that I would have been a good minister. However, God has given me gifts that allow me to minister to others. Not in a pulpit but in the everyday events of my life. The Bible entreats us to "be hospitable to one another without grumbling" (1 Peter 4:9). I intend to use my gifts to help others.

Scripture also says that we minister by our Christian example to others: "Let no man despise your youth; but be an example to those who believe, in word, in your way of life, in love, in spirit, in faith, and in purity." (1 Timothy 4:12). I have found that I struggle to set a good example of being a Christian. It's often easier for me to go along with popular opinions than to stand up for Christianity. I'm trying to be better at it.

I also still find it extremely difficult to share my beliefs with other people, especially strangers and even friends. I don't want them to think that I'm a "Bible beater," trying to force my beliefs on them. I find it awkward to share my beliefs, even in a one-to-one situation. Yet, I want to share the message of salvation. In my heart, I believe that is part of my assignment as a Christian.

I've thought about the gifts God has granted me. My marketing background may be the path to helping spread God's Word to others.

I've been blessed to experience marketing to millions of consumers. Perhaps I can communicate with them directly by using today's technology, media, and global reach.

Consequently, I have chosen to use my marketing background to reach people with a message of gratefulness. If I bring only one person to God through gratefulness, I feel I will have a better answer for God regarding how I have used my gifts to do for Him.

My hope is to bring the message of gratefulness to millions. I've also published the *Breakfast with God Grateful Journal* to provide an easy method of writing down seven items of gratefulness each day.

You may choose to dismiss this message, deeming me as a nutcase, that imagined I heard God's voice. But I have no doubt that God is real.

I can only relate my experience. Given the choice of believing or not believing, I personally bet on the believing side. When you are standing in front of God Almighty, wouldn't you rather risk eternity in heaven than in hell? God gave us free will, so it's up to each of us individually. You must decide which to choose. Each of us will face Him and be asked for an account of our lives. I've experienced that firsthand. I'm working on having a better answer next time I meet Him.

I will leave you with this final question. How will you answer when God asks:

What have you done with the talents that I gave you to do My work?

Appendix

Breakfast with God
Grateful Journal

This is a sample of the Grateful journal I developed. Starting on any day of any year, you can easily begin taking a few minutes each day to write seven things you are grateful for. This practice of gratitude will change your life!

January 2

Today, I'm grateful for:

1. _Your unconditional love and forgiveness_

2. _My promotion and pay raise_

3. _My son's acceptance to college_

4. _Successful surgery for my friend_

5. _Just for today's blessings_

6. _My granddaughter's 8th birthday_

7. _Your guidance on buying a new car_

Notes

You can order a copy of the *"Breakfast with God Grateful Journal,"* please email me at:

tom@gratefulministry.com

Other Resources

152 Bible Verses About Gratitude
https://stillfaith.com/topics/gratitude/

Gratitude List: 175+ Things to Be Grateful For
https://declutterthemind.com/blog/gratitude-list/

What is Sepsis?
https://www.nigms.nih.gov/education/fact-sheets/Pages/sepsis.aspx

Made in the USA
Middletown, DE
29 December 2022